DORSET IN A FORTNIGHT

BY

EDWARD R GRIFFITHS

A SPECIAL SERIES OF GUIDED WALKS
FOR AN INTIMATE EXPLORATION OF
THE BEST OF DORSET

INCLUDES A GAZETTEER OF PLACES VISITED

BOOK FOUR

BY THE SAME AUTHOR

THE STOUR VALLEY PATH   ISBN 0 9519376 1 8

"...the book is a gem which anybody...will add quickly and gratefully to their bookshelf" .....Dorset Life

THE CRANBORNE CHASE PATH   ISBN 0 9519376 2 6

"....combining exciting local colour with meticulous route information".....Greenlink Countryside Guide

"....the anecdotes and passionate descriptions will delight even those familiar with the Chase".....Western Gazette

THE BLACKMORE VALE PATH   ISBN 0 9519376 3 4

"....a walk to be savoured.   Happy rambling and enjoy Dorset".....Blackmore Vale Magazine

Clavell's Tower, Kimmeridge.   Page 90

© EDWARD R GRIFFITHS

ISBN 0 9519376 4 2

Published by Green Fields Books
13 Dalewood Avenue, Bear Cross
Bournemouth, BH11 9NR

DORSET IN A FORTNIGHT

CONTENTS

WALKS LOCATION MAP   ii

INTRODUCTION   1

KEY TO MAP SYMBOLS   3

1. THE KINGSTON LACY CIRCLE - 3 WALKS   5

2. THE SPREADEAGLE SAUNTER - 3 WALKS   32

3. THE STOUR VALLEY STROLL - 1 WALK   48

4. THE ABBOTSBURY AMBLE - 2 WALKS   56

5. THE ENCOMBE ENCOUNTER - 3 WALKS   75

6. THE MELBURY MEANDER - 3 WALKS   98

7. THE BOTTLEBUSH ROUND - 5 WALKS   120

IN CONCLUSION   148

BIBLIOGRAPHY AND ACKNOWLEDGMENTS   149

INDEX   150

PERSONAL LOG   154

DORSET IN A FORTNIGHT

WALKS LOCATION MAP

TITLE	WALKS	MILES
1. THE KINGSTON LACY CIRCLE	3	4.1/4 8.1/4 10.1/4
2. THE SPREADEAGLE SAUNTER	3	3.1/4 5.1.4 8.1/2
3. THE STOUR VALLEY STROLL	1	4.1/4
4. THE ABBOTSBURY AMBLE	2	3.3/4 8.1/4
5. THE ENCOMBE ENCOUNTER	3	5.1/2 6.3/4 9.1/4
6. THE MELBURY MEANDER	3	5.1/4 6.3/4 12
7. THE BOTTLEBUSH ROUND	5	5.1/4 5.1/2 6 8 13.1/2

DORSET IN A FORTNIGHT

INTRODUCTION

Whilst researching for the first three Green Fields Books which were published before this one - to be precise, *"The Stour Valley Path"*, *"The Cranborne Chase Path"* and *"The Blackmore Vale Path"* - I was frequently tempted to wander from my selected routes and to amble, willy-nilly, about this most beautiful of counties (keeping to Rights of Way, of course). If you have walked any, or all, of these first three long-distance paths, you will have experienced this same desire to find out where some of the adjacent Footpaths and Bridleways lead.

At the same time, I have been asked many times by Dorset bookshops whether I intend to produce any circular walks. My answer was always that I was trying to introduce long-distance walking routes for Dorset ramblers in much the same way as the rest of Britain appears to be covered, criss-crossed with official long-distance Paths such as the Coast to Coast Walk, The Pennine Way (both by dear old A W Wainwright), Offa's Dyke Path, The Cotswold Way and The Dales Way.

However, now that Book Three - *"The Blackmore Vale Path"* is in the shops, I have decided to complete this collection of 20 circular walks before embarking on any more long-distance paths. The areas have been specially chosen to reflect the diversity of landscape and the startling beauty of this wonderful county and, if you walk them all within a fortnight, you'll be exhausted but eager for more.

So, here they are. These Strolls, Meanders, Encounters or whatever are a miscellany of fine rambles, some whole days and some half days, which begin and end at the same spot, in country, town or village where you can park a car or where local buses are available. All are within the normal range of a reasonably fit person who can live without a huge meal or a couple of pints in the middle of the day (*but, before you set out, make sure I haven't given any dire warnings of steep hills which may cause you a problem*) If you load your backpack with just enough sandwiches and drinks to last until you get back - as well as your Ordnance Survey map, waterproofs and sun oil or extra jumpers (depending on which season you choose) - you'll be perfectly set for a wonderful, rewarding day out - and you don't really have to finish all the walks strictly within two weeks. Each walk is completely different from any of its companions in this book. If one takes you over hills and vales or along coastal paths, the next may take you through farming land or along a river. One may take you to a selection of small villages or a market town and manor house whilst another may lead you over chalk downs or along wooded tracks and ancient roads. Whichever you choose first, you won't be disappointed and, when you've tasted a few of the incomparable delights of Dorset, you'll be counting the days to your next excursion.

The maps are highly detailed, so you shouldn't have much trouble finding your way at any time but, if you happen to wander off, the relevant Ordnance Survey map which I recommend for each walk will soon bring you back.

Various bus companies serve the areas in which you will be walking but the most utilised will be Wilts and Dorset, Southern National and the many independent operators whose timetables are listed in the booklets entitled "Public Transport in Rural Dorset" and which are obtainable from Tourist Information Centres throughout Dorset. These timetables, which give full addresses of the operators, are also available direct from Dorset County Council, County Hall, Dorchester, DT1 1XT.

1

CIRCULAR WALKS IN THIS BOOK

Each walk begins with a description of the main features which you will meet during the day, together with the Map Reference for the starting point, the Ordnance Survey map/s which you should carry, parking areas available and any buses which will take you there. There are Mileage Tables which will enable you to plan your journey and the highly detailed Stage Maps show you how far you have come from the start. Follow the Maps but don't miss the adjacent text because that is where you'll find the extra details that will add to your enjoyment of the walk. On a few occasions, I recommend that you stop walking to read the text but this is only when I'm concerned that you may walk over a cliff edge or miss a special view because your head is stuck in the book.

Wherever possible, I have tried to make a figure-of-eight configuration of walks from the chosen start or offer a quick return alternative so that you can do a short circuit. Then, if you find that you have the time or suddenly feel that you aren't ready to go home yet, you can walk some more - and be sure that it'll be different from the walk that you've just finished.

RIGHTS AND RESPONSIBILITIES

All of the Footpaths, Bridleways, tracks and lanes have been followed very carefully on these walks and there were no insurmountable problems just before the completion of this book - although a couple of gates had to be climbed rather than opened because they were broken or damaged . However, if you should find a new obstruction on the correct route e.g. blocked, broken or wired-up gates or exits from fields, or lack of stiles, you should make a slight deviation and report the obstruction to the Rights of Way Section of the County Council. Such obstructions are illegal under Section 137 of the Highways Act 1980.

If you come across a ploughed field and the route crosses it or follows the edge of it, the Path or Bridleway has to be reinstated within 14 days of ploughing to widths of 1m and 2m respectively for the cross-field ways and 1.5m or 2.5m respectively for edgewise ways under the Rights of Way Act 1990. If these reinstatements have not been made, cross the field or follow the edge as you wish, whichever is easiest.

If you find a gate open, leave it open but, if it's closed, close it behind you - and don't drop litter. Observance of these two simple requests is all that is required to make the relationship between hiker and farmer perfectly harmonious so, with the delights of the open country awaiting you, get ready to go out and enjoy yourself.

I know I don't really need to remind you but, as with all of the other books, I feel it behoves me to tell you that you will be visiting working areas of Dorset - not one gigantic theme park or recreation area. Then again, if you come across someone ploughing, harvesting, woodcutting, dry-stone wall building, foresting or sheep herding (I've seen all of these on these walks), they won't usually mind if you stop and watch for a while. And one more thing (If you've read the other guides, you'll be expecting this) - call in at every village shop or post office that you find and buy something, even if you don't need it. These little shops need everybody's help to survive and it's all our fault because the supermarket chains have spread everywhere - and we use them - causing the village shops to close down from lack of custom. So, as you enjoy the beautiful Dorset countryside, give a bit back by helping to maintain the social life-blood of the villages - their shops.

2

KEY TO MAP SYMBOLS

ROUTE	
FOOTPATH OR BRIDLEWAY ARROW	
SIGNPOST	
HEDGE	
WIRE FENCE	
WOOD/IRON FENCE	
STONE/BRICK WALL	
STILE	
GATE - LARGE / GATE - SMALL	
BRIDGE OVER STREAM	
TREE - DECIDUOUS / TREE - PINE	
SPECIFIC BUILDING	
GROUP OF BUILDINGS - SCHEMATIC	
STREAM/RIVER	
EMBANKMENT/HILLSIDE (arrows point down)	
TUMULUS/BARROW	
CLIFF EDGE	
OVERHEAD CABLES	
MILES FROM START OF WALK	
ADJOINING MAP NUMBER	

Top: Melbury Sampford. Page 102

Bottom: Stour Provost. Page 52

PART ONE - THE KINGSTON LACY CIRCLE

INTRODUCTION

Using the popular market town of Wimborne Minster as the focal point, you have the opportunity to make a close inspection of the town and its surrounding farmland, the Iron-Age fort of Badbury Rings and to enjoy a 'beyond the pale' view of Kingston Lacy house. If you have travelled *"The Cranborne Chase Path"* you will be familiar with some parts of the routes described here - but not as circular, one-day routes. Options 1 and 2 begin in Wimborne so that the routes will be easy to follow and, when you reach the divergence of Routes 1 and 2, I will tell you what you will find either way. The shortest route (Route 3) uses part of Route 1 and part of Route 2 with a short connecting path along the beech avenue on the B3082. I'm sure you'll have no trouble following the instructions - No, really!

THE ALTERNATIVES

Starting outside the Minster Church of St Cuthburga (Reference SZ009999 on O S Map No. 195) or in the car park at Badbury Rings (Reference ST961032 on the same O S Map) on the B3082 between Wimborne and Blandford Forum, these round walks cover between 4.1/4 and 10.1/4 miles, depending on which option you choose.

ROUTE 1: Total distance 10.1/4 miles - This longest of the three Routes takes you through the centre of Wimborne, along the Northern road towards Cranborne and past Walford Mill. Field paths then take you past an ornate Victorian waterworks en route to High Hall (a miniature Kingston Lacy) before depositing you onto an easy country lane and farm tracks all the way to the "Druid oaks" of King Down Wood and Badbury Rings. A stroll along the beech avenue of the B3082 brings you to the track which circumnavigates Kingston Lacy Park and, after a tea stop at Pamphill, footpaths take you along the edge of the River Stour and the final leg into Wimborne.

ROUTE 2: Total distance 8.1/4 miles - This short cut from Route 1 misses out on Badbury Rings so I would only recommend it if you would rather visit the medieval hunting lodge of Lodge Farm than. Mind you, you could complete Route 1 and return for a shorter walk on Option 3, which also visits Lodge Farm, another time.

ROUTE 3: Total distance 4.1/4 miles - This shortest of walks begins and ends in the car park of Badbury Rings and, after a stroll along the B3082's beech avenue, visits Lodge Farm before joining the farm tracks on Routes 1 and 2 back to Badbury Rings.

By the way, there aren't any buses to get you to Badbury Rings so, unless you want to take your car and have a shorter walk, the longer routes are better because you start and finish in Wimborne which is served by innumerable buses. The buses which will get you to and from the the major towns are: - Poole - Wilts and Dorset 132, 133, X13 and Rural buses 333. Bournemouth - Wilts and Dorset 132, 133, 139, X13. Blandford and Shaftesbury - Wilts and Dorset 139 , X13 and Rural buses 333. Blandford, Poole, Bournemouth and Sturminster Newton - Wilts and Dorset 181

Once you've left Wimborne for the longer walks, you won't find any shops, tea-shops or pubs until you get to near the end. So pack a good lunch and go and enjoy the walk, promising yourself a rewarding tea or a stock of country provisions from the Pamphill Dairy Farm Shop. There are no shops at all on the shorter walk from Badbury Rings - although you may get an ice cream in the Car Park in the summer.

STAGE MILEAGES

STAGE	MILES	TOTAL MILES
ROUTE 1:		
1 Wimborne Minster to Walford	.50	.50
2 Walford to Catley Copse	.75	1.25
3 Catley Copse to High Hall	.75	2
4 High Hall to Barnsley Lane	1	3
5 Barnsley Lane to Bradford Path	1.25	4.25
6 Bradford Path to Badbury Rings	1.25	5.50
7 Badbury Rings to Beech Avenue	.75	6.25
8 Beech Avenue to Kingston Lacy Park	1.50	7.75
9 Kingston Lacy Park to Pamphill	.75	8.50
10 Pamphill to River Stour	1	9.50
11 River Stour to Wimborne Minster	.75	10.25
ROUTE 2:		
1 - 4 As Route 1 to Barnsley Lane	3	3
5 Barnsley Lane to Chilbridge Junction	.50	3.50
5a Chilbridge Junction to Lodge Farm	1.25	4.75
8 Lodge Farm to Kingston Lacy Park	1	5.75
9 - 11 As Route 1 to Wimborne Minster	2.50	8.25
ROUTE 3		
7 Badbury Rings to Beech Avenue	.75	.75
8 Beech Avenue to Lodge Farm	.50	1.25
5a Lodge Farm to Chilbridge Junction (Reverse Map)	1	2.25
5 Chilbridge Junction to Bradford Path	.75	3
6 Bradford Path to Badbury Rings	1.25	4.25

ROUTE LAYOUT

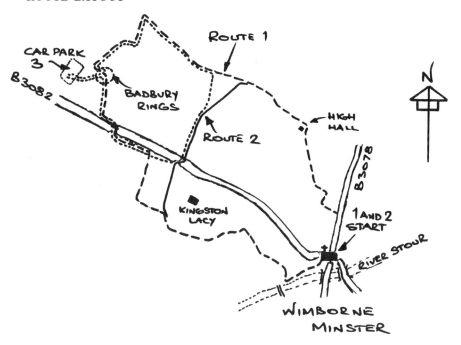

Kingston Lacy House. Page 26

STAGE 1

WIMBORNE MINSTER TO WALFORD

Before you set out from the glass-doored porch of the Minster Church of St Cuthburga, consider this:

Around 713 AD, a Benedictine nunnery was founded at what is now nearby Dean's Court by St Cuthburga, sister of Ina, King of the West Saxons and this Norman church with its mid-15thC West tower is built on the site of the abbey church which belonged to the nunnery. By that time, Wimborne was already an important settlement known as Wymburn or Winburnham because of its position on the banks of the River Wym where it joined the River Stour,

In 871 AD, after the battle with the invading Danes at Martin, near Cranborne, King Alfred the Great buried his fatally wounded brother Ethelred here.

Above your left shoulder, you will see the Quarter Jack who was carved in 1613 as a monk. However, since the Napoleonic wars he has sported the livery of a Grenadier. He is connected to an entirely separate mechanism from the amazing astronomical clock inside the church and he has to be wound up every day.

You really should make a point of visiting this church to see the chained library, the Saxon chest, the Man in the Wall and the Uvedale monument - all as detailed in the Minster's "Guide for Pilgrims and Visitors".

Time to go now so, straight ahead, leave the churchyard and cross over Cooks Row, past the toilets and on across Cornmarket into Church Street. After the "Oddfellow Arms", cross over West Street at the traffic lights, with The Square on your right and The King's Head on your left, and continue along West Borough. The Tivoli Cinema (and theatre), which you will soon pass on the left, was a fine 18thC house until its conversion into a cinema in the 1930s. It was abandoned in the 1970s and it lay neglected and unloved until restoration was begun in 1993 by the Tivoli Trust.

After the traffic lights at the junction with Priors Walk and Hanham Road, keep on past the Town Council's offices and School Lane on your left. Cross over to the right as your pavement runs out in a minute. Then, past Chapel Lane and the Stone Lane traffic lights, cross over East Borough to Walford Bridge where the River Allen flows. Opposite East Borough is Knobcrook Lane which leads to a fine 18thC converted flour mill which is now the Walford Mill Craft Centre. This mill warrants a return visit to view the constantly changing exhibitions by invited local artists, craftsmen and women together with the work of resident designers of textiles, ceramics, wood, jewellery, glass and metalwork. All in all, you could spend some very happy hours in Wimborne. There is a superb Market every Friday with smaller versions on Saturdays and Sundays. Go and visit the Tourist Information Centre in the High Street and they'll make sure you have a good time - but not today.

Now, cross over the bridge and continue out of Wimborne, passing the "Crown and Anchor" Inn on the other side of the road and with a field on your side.

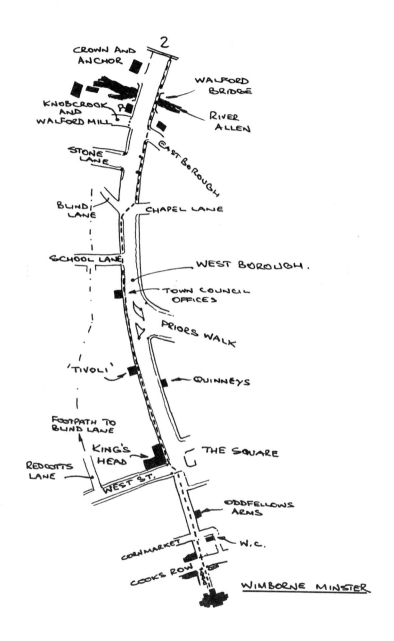

STAGE 2

WALFORD TO CATLEY COPSE

After Minster Garage on your left and before Shakespeare Road on your right, cross back over the main Cranborne road and turn onto the farm track which is signposted "Public Footpath - High Hall". Go through the kissing gate or, at your own risk, carefully cross the cattle grid and follow the track past two houses on your left and with a wire-fenced, open field on your right.

After the barns on your left, the ground dips on the left to a hedge and some trees. This leads you to a "squeeze" stile and a farm gate as the track bears left. The RH gates lead into the Wimborne Pumping Station and you will have a clearer view of the Victorian works in a few moments. The painted yellow arrow on the gatepost and the "Footpath" arrow on the stile confirm that you should keep to this track and follow the RH hedge between you and the Pumping Station.

Beyond the trees on your right, there is a high grass bank which probably forms a side of a water storage tank whilst, over on your left, a couple of wire fences show where the River Allen is flowing towards Walford Mill and Bridge. Now, look back to the Pumping Station. What a glorious, ivy-clad structure for what is purely a utility building. Those Victorians certainly had style - like it or not - and they built things to last in those days.

As the track bears round to the right, pass through the narrow, Footpath-arrowed opening by the side of the farm gate on your right and follow the RH edge of the uphill field, past another opening into the RH field and past two cattle troughs against the fence. At the top RH corner of this field, there is a conglomeration of signs and arrows ensuring that you keep to the right path. There are yellow arrows on two posts, a large white arrow on the sign "Please Keep Dogs on Leash" and a "Private Woods - Keep Out" notice. Do what you're told and turn left to follow the edge of Catley Copse (for so it is called) down the field to the gate in the hedge facing you at the bottom.

On your way down the field, you will see High Hall in the trees some way ahead of you and Badbury Rings, with the thin woods on top, up on the horizon in the front left distance.

Keep going, uphill now, past the RH gate into the Copse, again signed "Private Woods - Keep Out", until you reach the far end of the woods and the field opens out on your right. Cross over the open field, aiming for the electricity pylon ahead of you, a few fields away, and with the track bearing right, uphill, towards Wilksworth Caravan Park. Keep straight on, not following the main track, and climb over the stile in the wire fence facing you. Here again you are instructed to "Keep Dogs on Leash" whilst a Footpath arrow points straight ahead to an indistinct path in the next field. Those signs keep reminding me of the problem caused to people without dogs who come across the notice "Dogs Must be Carried on the Escalator" I suppose they could always use the stairs - or borrow a dog.

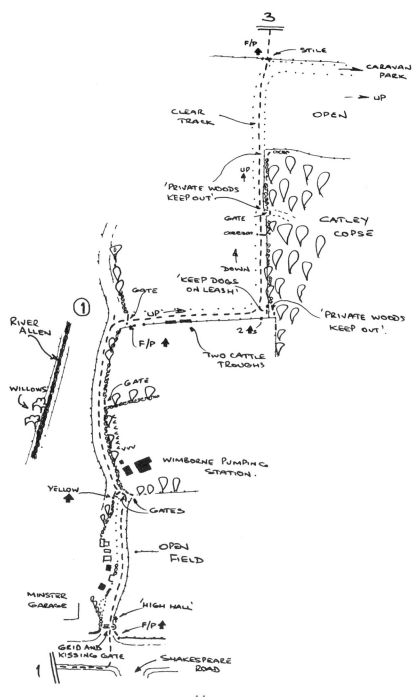

STAGE 3

CATLEY COPSE TO HIGH HALL

Across this field, climb over the Footpath-arrowed stile into a narrow wood.   A two-sleepers wide by 50 ft (15 and a bit metres) long walkway leads you through the wood, keeping you out of the bog.   Climb over the stile in the fence on the other side and keep straight on, aiming just to the right of the RH leg of the electricity pylon in this field.

On the far side of the field, cross the track which straddles your path and climb over the stile in the fence and hedge into the next field.   All of these stiles have Footpath arrows, so your direction is quite clear.   Now, aim straight for High Hall as you go down this wide field to the stile on the left of the farm gate at the bottom.

More arrows here and on the bridge across the River Allen, which is in the next field, point you towards the Hall.   Over the bridge, be sure not to veer right towards the ditch bridge in this field.   I did and suddenly I was surrounded by cows and up to my fetlocks in sodden grass.   Instead, follow the fence on your left to its end, going over a brick tunnel which carries the ditch water under your path, and into the next open field.

Cross the open field to an arrowed stile which leads into a strip of wood.   This narrow wood sits in a dip and it is only 35 yds (about 11 metres - and I can't keep up this E.C. correctness for the whole book) until you leave it over the stile on the other side.   Now, before leaving this stile, look carefully up the next field and aim for the farm gate which stands just a little to the left up on the hill ahead of you, with a pair of fine oaks close to the top fence on the right.   On your way up, you go past the RH edge of a small, fenced wood and, on your arrival at the gate, two painted Footpath arrows confirm that you are still alright.

Go through the gate, remembering to close it behind you as there are usually some very smart ponies grazing in this field.   By the way, avoid eye contact with the ponies or they may become over-friendly.   I have often found that ponies of this ilk have a penchant for leaning on human beings and, with the somewhat unfortunate weight differential, their affection can propel the inferior human earthwards at quite a rate.   Anyway, follow the perimeter hedge and fence of High Hall's garden and tennis court on your left.

On your way past, take a surreptitious look at the Hall, within the bounds of etiquette of course, and try to remember something of its style for later in the day when you'll have a similar view of High Hall's bigger relation, Kingston Lacy.

I'll tell you more about Kingston Lacy when you get there but, for now, a little potted history will suffice - John Bankes had six daughters and a son, Ralph Bankes, who built Kingston Lacy. The youngest daughter, Arabella, married a Samuel Gilly and this gentleman built High Hall in about 1670 as a smaller version of Kingston Lacy which was completed only five years earlier.   No doubt, his bride would have felt much at home here.   By descent, High Hall passed to John Fitch who made his fortune in public works after the 1666 Great Fire of London.   He passed his skills on to William, his son, who was also a builder of repute and whose many achievements included the construction of the South aisle of Wimborne Minster.

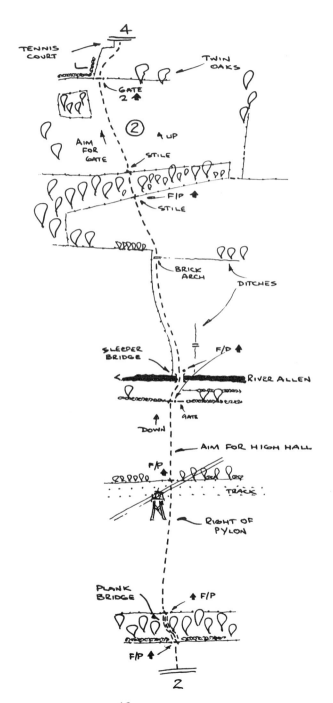

STAGE 4

HIGH HALL TO BARNSLEY LANE

Keep close to the fence, passing a gate which leads into the rear drive of High Hall, and then climb over the stile in the LH wire fence near to some gnarled and twisted oaks. A Footpath arrow points towards the entrance gates to the front drive. Head quietly towards them and leave High Hall by the small gate or, carefully, over the cattle grid. As you crossed the stile, a glance towards the house would have shown you a wood-clad water tower in the trees near to the house. This tower looks something like the turret of a Bavarian castle.

Now, outside on the tarmac lane, with a row of trees in High Hall's grounds on your left and with a farm track and a triplicity of gates opposite, turn left and begin a pleasant, easy walk along the lane with trees and hedges all around. Because of the age of these trees, there is usually a variety of bird song accompanying this stroll.

Past a few gates into the fields to left and right and a track into the wood on your right, you arrive at a RH bend in the lane which acquires a wide verge and a ditch on the left and a beech hedge alongside the wood on your right. Continuing up the lane, go past two cottages on your right and a few more gates in the hedges.

The next turning on the right, with the banked hedge just opposite a post box, is signed for "Barnsley Farm". Don't turn off but prepare yourself for a long, slow uphill walk of about 3/4 mile along the straight lane. With ditches and verges on both sides, go past Lower Barnsley Cottages, Barnsley House with its tennis court, past a small barn against the LH hedge and the turning off to "Lower Barnsley Farm", again on your left. Keep on going and, with large fields on both sides, up on the horizon to your left is King Down Wood which hides Badbury Rings from your view.

High Hall. Page 14

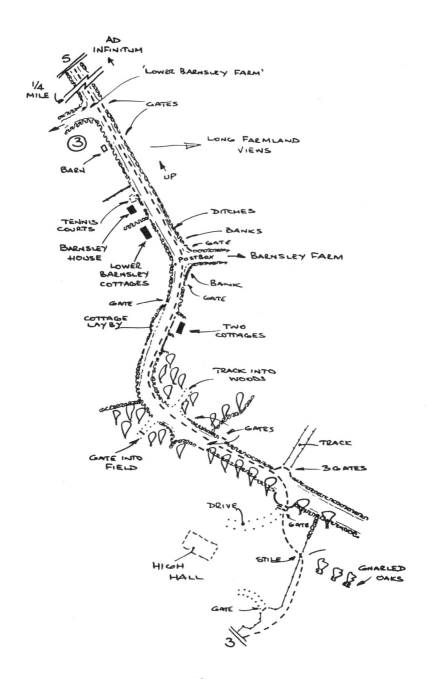

15

BARNSLEY LANE TO BRADFORD PATH (and Chilbridge Junction)

Keeping on up this lane, counting the gates to pass the time, you will arrive eventually at a junction of farm tracks.   Before this, however, if you look carefully into the distant trees on your left, you should be able to make out the white cupola up on the roof of Kingston Lacy.   You'll be there within the next couple of hours.

Now, passing the two gates at the end of the lane, wander into an open junction area where all of the farm tracks have wide verges.   Clockwise, the first left track goes down to Chilbridge Farm, a truly ancient establishment which belonged to Alcester Abbey in the Middle Ages.   It is built close to an ancient crossing of the River Allen flood plains and derives its name from the Old English 'ceole' and 'bryeg' meaning the bridge over the channel.   Whichever way you go from here, you cannot help but notice the great width of the farm tracks.   These date back to when Chilbridge Farm was devoted to sheep and the wide tracks made sheep movements easier.   It is now almost entirely devoted to barley, pig and dairy production.   The next track goes to Lodge Farm and this is the turning for the shorter Route 2 which will save you 2 miles from the day's walk.   However, now that you're here, it would be better not to miss Badbury Rings, wouldn't it - and the wonderful, extensive views from the top of this Iron age hill fort are much too spectacular to miss.

ROUTE 2: If your mind is made up to visit Lodge Farm today - and to cut 2 miles off your journey - turn off here and follow the Stage 5a map.

ROUTE 1: For Badbury Rings, follow the main track past the gate in the corner of the LH fenced field and past an open silage area which is backed by a sparse hedge on your right.   After the open area, the track descends, narrower and stonier, between fenced fields, to another distant junction.

In the field on your left, known as King Down, you will see two distinct tumuli, the first of many on this Route.   *Route 3 crosses this field from Stage 5a - Don't you!* In fact, the next stretch is alive with the memories of Iron age and Bronze age men and the Roman invaders who overtook their homes and their culture.

However, just keep on going down and you will arrive at opposing Bridleway-signed gates astride the track.   The LH track goes up to and past the tumuli to rejoin the Lodge Farm track on Route 2.   After the gates, you arrive at the junction where "*The Cranborne Chase Path*" turns right on its way to Salisbury.   For today, follow the zig-zag track straight ahead, past the small LH copse and the facing RH gate.   There is grass up the middle of the track as the stony track leads uphill between the LH hedge and the RH fenced field.   On the way, you pass a pair of very wide gates and a stunted oak on the left and a gate into the RH field.   At the top of the track, the "tumulus" in the field on your right is really a grass covered water tank and, with the track now enclosed by hedges, you begin a short descent with good long views straight ahead and over on your right towards Manswood and Witchampton.

On the way down, go past the two gates which cross the track and the two gates into the side fields.   Now levelling out, you arrive at a turning to the right with a house on the RH corner.   Keep straight on, past the field gate on your left and the hedged garden on your right and turn straight to Stage 6 - ignoring 5a on the next page.

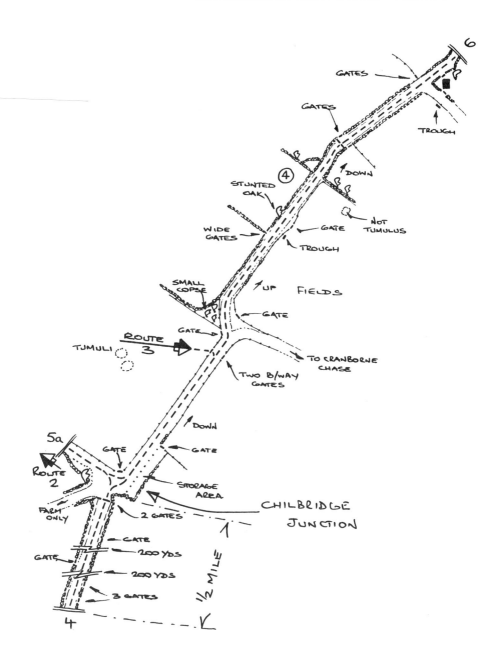

CHILBRIDGE JUNCTION TO LODGE FARM (both directions)

ROUTE 3 - *Don't forget to follow this Map in reverse and cross the tumuli field.*

ROUTE 2: Having left the Route 1 walkers to carry on to Badbury Rings, follow the straight, gravel track with a ditch in the LH verge and a wire fenced field on your right. Level at first, then descending very slightly, the track bends left at a RH gate with three Bridleway arrows. The RH field Bridleway leads to two distinct tumuli, about 100 yards away at the top of the field. With the verge widths varying on right and left, follow the track past a LH gate at the bottom of the incline and back up to another gate in the LH hedge just before a bend takes you round a fenced concrete enclosure and a three-part barn (Dutch in the middle with two lean-tos).

After the barn, you reach a wide, rough grassy area on your left with an old shed and with the fenced field still on your right. Another farm track crosses your way here, with a horse-jump in the wire fence facing you. The track to the left again leads to Chilbridge Farm whilst the right direction leads to King Down Woods and Farm (but both are private farm tracks). Zig-zag left and right to the other side and join the continuing level track with the wider verge and a hedge on the LH side and another fenced field on the right. Keep on, with slow ascents and descents, along the track with grass up the middle, around a right bend with a LH gate and past a few, ivy-clad ash trees in the LH hedge.

The track bends right again as you ascend slightly, past a small wood of old beech trees and along a short section of tarmac, to arrive at a gate and half a gate just before the B3082 Wimborne to Blandford road. Emerging onto a very wide verge with a 2-way Bridleway signpost, turn right and follow the wide green track with the road on your left and the wire-fenced field on your right. On the other side of the road, you will see a fine, stone Lodge with a pair of stone pillars and wrought iron gates which lead onto a drive to Kingston Lacy House. This drive was a continuation of the majestic avenue of beeches which runs for two miles ahead of you and past Badbury Rings but now the B3082 bends here and runs around the Eastern edge of Kingston Lacy Park and past the more modern, un-Lodged, entrance.

Anyway, at the end of the RH field, the drive on your right leads to the 14thC Lodge Farm which, at about the time of the Peasants' Revolt, was a hunting lodge for the Manor of Kingston Lacy. Apart from its superbly preserved architectural features inside, excavations have revealed many personal items which belonged to the 17thC occupants, the Short family. These include many domestic items - and a mould which was used to forge shilling coins of William III. There are fascinating artefacts displayed here, including Neolithic, Bronze and Iron age items excavated nearby.

However, cross over the drive and continue along the track, past a low barrier. After the first couple of beech trees which line the road, bear left on a faint path and cross over to the track opposite which leads into the car park for visitors to Lodge Farm.

Now turn directly to Stage 8 and follow your particular part of the Stage 8 map which leads you along the undulating Bridleway from the car park, with the bird-filled beech woods surrounding Kingston Lacy Park on your left and with fields and a wood on your right. After about 1/2 mile, you meet up with the Route 1 walkers at Sweetbriar Drive on your right, with a 3-way Bridleway signpost on the junction.

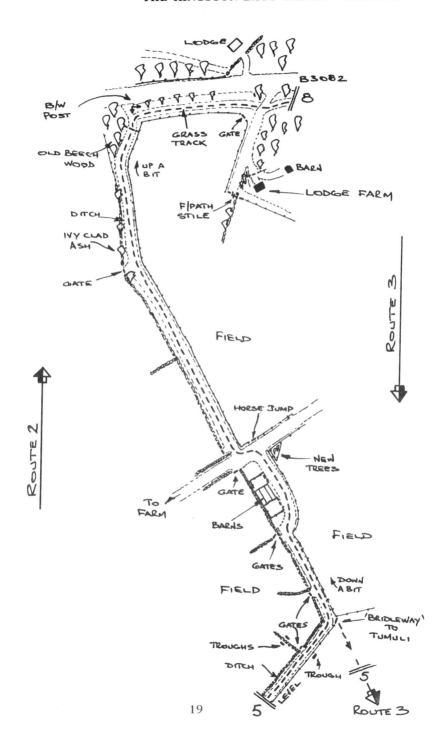

STAGE 6

BRADFORD PATH TO BADBURY RINGS

At the left bend in the farm track, the wide grassy area on your right is where the Footpath from *"The Cranborne Chase Path"* returns on the line of the Roman Ackling Dyke military road from Old Sarum (pre-Salisbury) to Badbury Rings, after 5 days wandering through the delights of the Chase. Ignore the Bridleway-arrowed gate facing you and turn left to follow the wide gravel track that is Ackling Dyke uphill with hedges and grass verges on both sides. At the top of the track, the line of the Dyke goes straight on, invisibly, into the woods whilst the farm track continues down to King Down Farm.

With two farm gates over on your left, turn right into the woods and follow the Bridleway's meanderings, never far from the wire fence of the field on your right. In "The Old Roads of Dorset", Ronald Good recalls that these old woods, called "The Oaks" are "of immense age, bowed and hollow, and festooned with lichens and ferns". They are known locally as "Druid Oaks" but this merely confirms their great age. In the early 16thC, that great traveller Leland visited "the famous wood of Bathan, near Badbury Rings" so, in the steps of the famous, follow the path through the tangled, mysterious wood. After a cantilever gate into a field on the right, you eventually arrive at a junction of tracks where you need to zig-zag left and right. Over the farm gate just a little right at this junction, you have your first view of the long beech avenue which runs along the B3082 to one of the old lodge gates of Kingston Lacy.

On the last stretch of wooded Bridleway, you soon emerge on the far side of the wood onto a grassy, descending track between wire-fenced fields.

On the way down, you will see Badbury Rings earthworks up on the left - suddenly very close after being hidden for so long. When the track reaches the bottom of the dip and has passed a gated and overgrown shrubbery on your right and confirmation Bridleway arrows, you arrive in a narrow thicket of trees and scrub. Ignore any narrow paths which run up to the left as you pass around the gate but, when you emerge onto the grassier slopes beyond, turn instantly left, uphill, between this dense scrub and a couple of hawthorns. Follow the edge of this "Conservation Area' and cross the grassy track which emerges from the gate on your left.

Past a tumulus on the right, keep straight on up the slope to a wooden gate in the fence which crosses your path. *If you have a dog with you, the notice indicates that you will have to go around the perimeter fence of the Rings to join the main B3082 and turn left to meet the dog-less at the exit stile which is shown on your Stage 7 guide map.* Everybody else, climb over the gate and look for the Ordnance Survey column on the inner ring to your left. Aiming generally for this column, head for the staircase up the slope of the outer ring and crossing over the track which is the Ackling Dyke as it approaches the outer edge of Badbury Rings and continues past it to Maiden Castle - another, bigger Roman-occupied hill fort just outside Dorchester (Durnovaria).

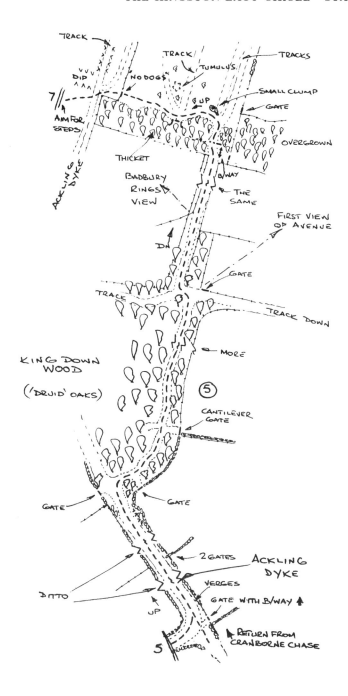

STAGE 7

BADBURY RINGS TO BEECH AVENUE

ROUTE 1: To reduce the erosion of this important site, the National Trust has built a series of inconspicuous steps into the embankments and I implore you to use them on your way to the O.S. column.   The Stage map shows that the most direct route over the Rings actually leads you away from the O.S. column, towards the right, so go that way and double back towards the column when you reach the top of the inner ring.   Take your time to enjoy the views and to feel the magic of this historic site and, when you reach the column, rest awhile and I'll tell you something of the Rings.

Badbury Rings encloses an area of 14 acres whilst the central ring, with a depth of 40ft, measures 1 mile in circumference.   Built in the Stone age, it was occupied successively by Bronze age, Iron Age, Roman and Saxon settlers - all of whom would have been contained within high wooden palisades built upon the rings.   Named after Bada, the local chief of the Durotriges, Badbury Rings succumbed to the Roman invaders under Vespasian in the early days of the invasion of South-West England which began with the fall of the Isle of Wight (Vectis) in AD 45.   This camp was strategically placed on the main trading routes from (using the modern names) Poole, Dorchester, Exeter, Salisbury and onwards to London.

Now, turn back along the inner ring for a few yards, then turn towards the centre, along the grass path between the old oaks.   Head up between the fenced pine enclosures to the information plinth which marks the dead centre of the Rings.

ROUTE 3: *Having just arrived from the Car Park, your walk begins here.*

ROUTES 1 AND 3: The plinth is aligned with its corners facing North, South, East and West.   When you have studied the map on top and tried to pick out a few selected spots, leave the plinth and walk down the South avenue.

Having descended to the top of the inner ring again, study the grassland down below you and you will see a definite, and ancient, grass track which leaves the Rings and heads towards the avenue of beech trees along the main road facing you.   Keep this track in mind and turn right for 50-60 yds along the top of the ring for the best route off the Rings, using steps where these are provided.   On the green track, follow it across open ground which is filled with molehills and hawthorn bushes until you reach the fence which encloses the Rings site.   The green track ends at the fence but go over the stile about 10 yds away on your right out onto an immensely wide verge between you and the ancient avenue of beeches which are lining the Wimborne to Blandford road.   The small beech trees in the iron cages will replace the existing avenue when it becomes too expensive to preserve - or when a wider road is decreed. They are constantly being treated by tree surgeons and the cost to the National Trust must be enormous.   Of course, when they were planted, they were to line a drive to Kingston Lacy and a few twigs or branches falling off wouldn't have been the same problem as if they were to drop onto a car or truck doing 60 mph along the B3082.

Now, turn left and follow the wide verge, past the RH turning to Sturminster Marshall and past the car parking area where 1.1/2 gates lead onto the signed Bridleway on the left.   After the car park, keep on for a few more yards and, just after the T-junction sign over on the other side of the road, carefully cross over to the equally wide RH verge at the point with the longest, safest view of the on-roaring traffic.

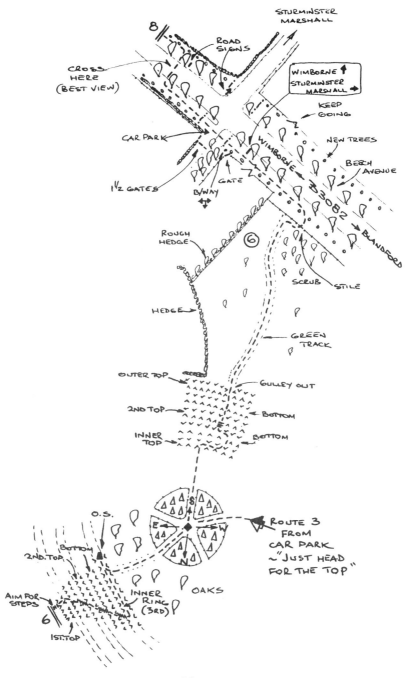

STAGE 8

BEECH AVENUE TO KINGSTON LACY PARK (and Lodge Farm)

Everybody safely on the other side - go to the wooden gate in the RH hedge 20 yds from the " 200 yds to the Junction" sign and choose your Route.

ROUTE 3: *Don't go through the gate but continue along this verge for another 1/4 mile and cross back to the LH side when you reach the Car Park. From there, turn to Stage 5a and follow the Map in reverse. It's not as complicated as you think.*

ROUTE 1: Go through the gate, leaving the wide verge and the traffic and entering a wide, grassy track between fenced open fields.   All of the land around Badbury Rings, Shapwick village, Kingston Lacy and almost into Wimborne itself was left to the National Trust in a massive bequest by the Bankes Estate in 1985 and also included the vast Bankes Estate lands around Corfe Castle in Purbeck.   Here, at Kingston Lacy, the 7000 acre estate includes the 250 acre wooded park around which you will shortly be walking.   Keep following this grassy track, pleasantly between new fenced hedges and slightly downhill, to a zig-zag at the bottom.   After a dip around an older hawthorn hedge, the track begins to climb up again.   Usually, the peace of this track is broken by the squabbling of crows and rooks in the trees over on your right and this cacophony frequently drowns the more musical song of the great variety of the smaller birds who have made their homes in Kingston Lacy Park. Anyway, up and down, past an intruding piece of hedge on the way up, you go past a replanted wood on your left at the top of the rise.   At the end of the track, a wired opening leads into the field on your right where one large and one small gate lead you onto an old Bridleway known as Sweetbriar Drove.   A 3-way Bridleway post points along all of the tracks but you turn left here.   The hedge now on your right contains many beech, oak and ash trees but these have recently been supplemented by replanted specimens.

Over this hedge, you can look down into the Stour Valley.   Actually, you are now on part of *"The Stour Valley Path"*, the 60 miles long guided walk from Christchurch to the source of the River Stour at Stourhead which was the subject of my very first long-distance walk book in 1994.   You will soon come across some Dorset County Council "Stour Valley Way" signs but these are not the same as *"The Stour Valley Path"*.   In 1995, Dorset County Council opened the first stage of their own version of a path along the Stour, as far as Sturminster Marshall, just across the Stour from here, but *"The Stour Valley Path"* already leads you on the complete, fascinating journey along the Stour - all the way to its source at Stourhead.   However, keep following Sweetbriar Drove, past many gates, openings and "Private" tracks, to a T-junction at its end.   With a 3-way Bridleway post, near to a "Private" gate which leads into Kingston Lacy Park, turn right.

ROUTE 2: *(the short-cut which missed Badbury Rings) Rejoin Route 1 after crossing the B3082 from Lodge Farm and following the wide, grassy track from the Car Park on this side.*

ROUTES 1 AND 2: Follow the clear, stony track with a ditch before the woods on the left and with a hedge on the right, negotiating an overhanging beech tree on the way.   At the next LH corner, another wide green track goes off to the right with the first indication of the "Stour Valley Way", but just keep following the main track around the Park.

24

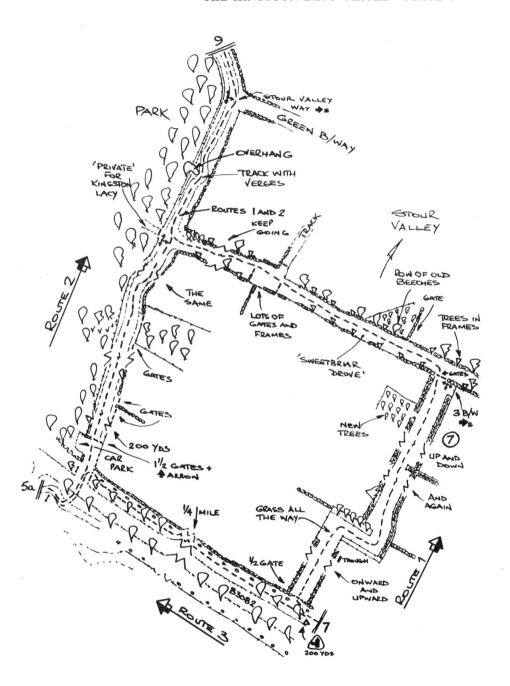

KINGSTON LACY PARK TO PAMPHILL

The vast estates of Kingston Lacy and Corfe Castle were bought by Sir John Bankes, Chief Justice in Charles I's time, between 1632 and 1635. The house was built by his son, Sir Ralph Bankes (the one whose sister resided in High Hall), between 1663 and 1665 by the architect Sir Roger Pratt. During the Commonwealth (the reign of Parliament and Cromwell), both Bankes and Pratt spent a lot of time on the continent, out of harms way, but, at the restoration of the monarchy, Sir Ralph built this house. Originally of brick, the entire building was encased with Chilmark stone for Sir Ralph's grandson, William, by his friend and architect, Charles Barry, between 1835 and 1840. William later went to live in Italy, from where he sent marble fittings and Italian woodwork back to Kingston Lacy, until his death in 1855. It was William's grandson, Sir Ralph Bankes, who bequeathed the Estates to the National Trust in 1985.

Now, after that potted history and making a mental note to come and enjoy the house and grounds another day, keep following the track for another 1/2 mile, past several "Private" gates into the woods on your left and with hedged fields on your right. A ditch appears first on your left and later on your right. Just after two openings into the RH fields, there is an estate cottage on your left which has a small, but beautifully kept, garden. Just after the cottage and the "Strictly Private" gate after it, you arrive at the "South Lodge Car Park" with an access barrier across your track. You will find another Stour Valley Way sign on the corner and, although you are on your way to Pamphill, don't follow the direction sign down to the right with the pines on the roadside bank.

Keep straight on up the tarmac lane, Abbot Street, with the ornately-gated gardens on the right where produce for the "big house" was grown, past the greenhouses and onwards, next past two more cottages dated 1907 and the field beyond. All this time, the encircling woods are still over on your left. On the next bend, a gate opens onto a farm track which leads up to the red-brick outbuildings and barns of Manor Farm whilst another gated track leads down to the National Trust woodyard in the trees on your left.

You are still skirting around "Manor Farm" whilst the next LH track leads into the Park past a couple of low sheds. On the bend in the road, the next two gates lead onto drives to Manor Farm's outbuildings and the lane then begins to ascend between higher banks. There is a cottage either side of the LH turning, high up on hedged banks, whilst there are some fine old oaks in the field up on your right. The first cottage stands on the line of a Roman road from Badbury Rings which crosses your path here.

At the top of this gulley, the old red-brick blacksmith's forge stands squarely against the roadside on your right. This is closely followed by Forge Cottage and another hedged cottage with a thatched summer house on the corner. If you had followed the Stour Valley Way sign from the car park down the lane, you would have been returning to our route up the track past this summer house. This is All Fools Lane and it leads down to Cowgrove - away from our route. You can see where walkers on the Stour Valley Way (not Path) have cut across the verge to go down All Fools Lane. Now, keep straight on up the lane for a few more yards, still with the woods on your left and a field hedge on your right.

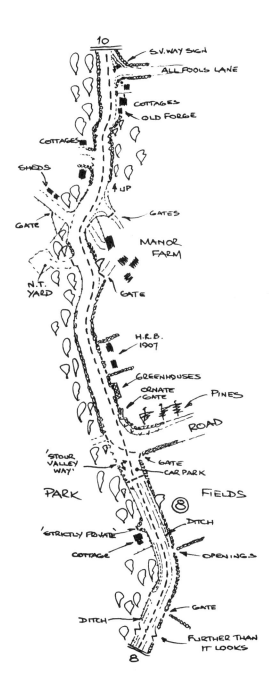

PAMPHILL TO RIVER STOUR

Just past All Fools Lane, the road continues around a slight LH bend, passing the white gated entrance to St Stephen's Church on its way to the Pamphill Dairy Farm Shop. You can get a nice cup of tea in the Tea Rooms there or a snack from the Shop to bring away with you if you would like to rest awhile on a bench by the Pamphill Cricket Pitch.. Either now or when you return from the Shop, turn right through the low wooden posts and follow the straggly path through the trees. Cross a small ditch with the railway-sleeper bridge and you will be in a gravel car parking area signed "National Trust - Pamphill Green".

This village green dates back to the 13thC and was the site of the fairs which were granted to the lords of Kingston Lacy. The superb avenue of oaks was planted in 1846 and it leads straight to St Stephen's Church. However, the church wasn't built until 1907, the same year as the two cottages which you passed on the right after South Lodge Car Park. It is in the late decorated style, by C E Ponting, and its details are influenced a great deal by the Arts and Crafts movement of that period. Over on your left there is a collection of farm cottages including the rather unusual 18thC thatched Pamphill Farmhouse with its ornamental caps on the chimneys and with an added, castellated porch. Beyond the car park, behind the hedge at the end of an elevated track, lies the superb late 17thC Pamphill Manor House. This was built by Matthew Beethall, steward to Sir Ralph Bankes, and a fine stable block was added to the right of the house in the 18thC.

Now, carry on along the grass to the right of the Oak Avenue and, when you arrive at the edge of the cricket pitch, you will find a bench beneath the old oak tree, facing the thatched 1909 cricket pavilion. Late on a summer evening, there probably isn't a better place to be in all England, with a village cricket match drawing to its close - especially if you have a little something from the Farm Shop to nibble on.

At the end of the avenue, go past the anti-car barriers and an array of gates on the right and follow the road past Pamphill Village School which was built in 1698 by Roger Gillingham as a school and almshouse. After the Stour Valley Way marker, which is opposite a lane coming in from your right around the edge of the lesser Little Pamphill Green, skirt around the LH bushes and, just before the first cottage on Vine Hill, turn sharp left and cross the grassy area to an electricity pylon. You could have kept straight on down the road to the Vine Inn but your chances of being run over would have been considerable - and, if you go the pretty way, you may see a woodpecker or some jays. Directly underneath the pylon, bear right by the 3-way Footpath signpost and drop down some steps between bushes to the first of several squeeze-stiles. Through the stile, follow the path down to the left, with an embankment on your right and a few trees, a ditch and a fenced field on your left. More steps bring you to a junction of paths and, ignoring all others, take the RH signed Footpath, along a row of trees and with the bank up on your right.

A stream runs along on your left and, after the next stile, you cross open ground, with a wooden fence on your right, to cross over this stream with a plank bridge and another stile. Turn right after the Stour Valley Way signpost and follow the edge of the stream through this field. Over the stile at the end of the field, turn right onto the Cowgrove road, then go over the next stile in the LH hedge, opposite Vine Hill, into the field with a hedge and ditch on your left.

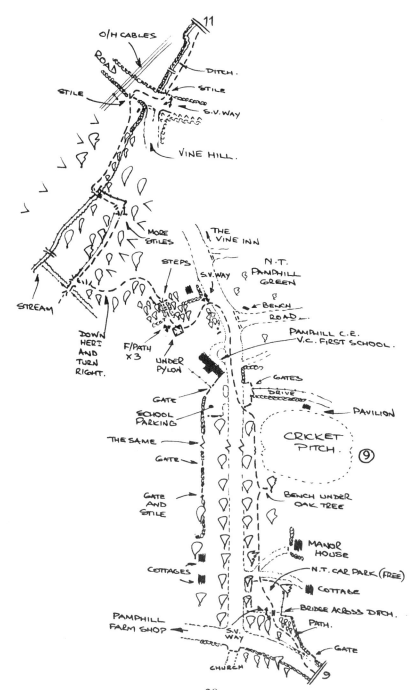

29

STAGE 11

RIVER STOUR TO WIMBORNE MINSTER

Heading towards the River, cross over the stream on the left, using the signed footbridge and the squeeze-stile.   In this next field, keep following the wide grass path to the next stile with another bridge across a ditch.   On the River bank, there is a magnificent willow tree with long branches gracefully hanging from its vast bulk.

Keep straight on, ignoring another path which bears off to your left, and follow the short fence to the corner of the facing hedge, beyond which a singularly unused stile stands at the end of a broken wire fence.   With the fence on your left, and with football pitches on the other side, go past a fenced surface water outfall and, between hawthorns and a few small trees, you emerge into some allotments with a track coming from your left.   Aim for the Minster which you will see directly ahead of you and don't turn off the track at all.   At its end, a Footpath sign points back to Eye Bridge which is just a little upstream from where you joined the Riverside path.   Eye Bridge stands next to an ancient, and still used, ford crossing which is close to the point where the Roman road from Badbury Rings crossed the Stour on its way to Moriconium (now Hamworthy, Poole).

When you leave the allotments and join a tarmac road with a block of flats on your right, follow the road around to the left, between townhouses and garages, past the Pay and Display car park on the left and the small factory unit on the right.   In a few yards, you reach the B3082 Wimborne to Blandford Road where it is still called Victoria Road.   There is another Pay and Display car park on the left corner of Old Road as you leave it.

Now, be very careful!   Wimborne is usually very busy and you've been away from the hurly-burly of everyday life for most of today.

Cross Victoria Road and turn up West Street, past the "Pudding and Pye" on Pye Corner, past a garage and a few small shops and houses along the road.   Where the road bends around to the left, turn into the lane on your right.   Just ahead is the old Wesleyan Chapel and, bearing left and right, you arrive in Cornmarket.   In this pedestrianized area, close to the "White Hart Inn", there are plenty of benches but you're nearly there now.   So stroll into Cooks Row and turn onto the Minster path where the glass porch doors are waiting to welcome you back after a lovely day's rambling.

Don't forget to come back again to Wimborne Minster and Kingston Lacy.   You'll have a great day or two amidst the grandeur of Kingston Lacy and its Park and around the fine, historic town of Wimborne Minster.   There's plenty to see.

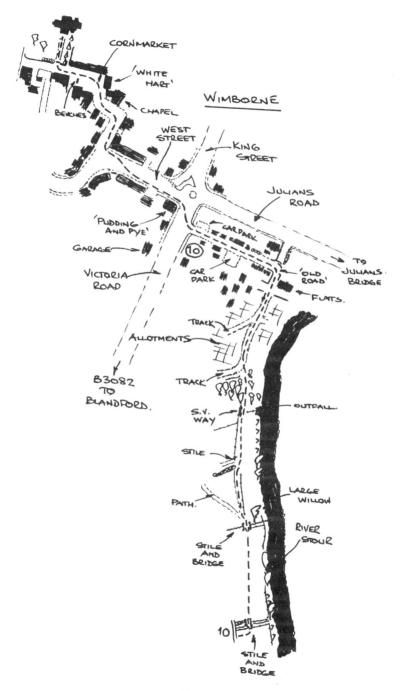

CORNMARKET

'WHITE HART'

CHAPEL

BENCHES

WIMBORNE

WEST STREET

KING STREET

JULIANS ROAD

'PUDDING AND PYE'

CAR PARK

GARAGE

10

VICTORIA ROAD

CAR PARK

'OLD ROAD'

TO JULIANS BRIDGE

FLATS.

TRACK

ALLOTMENTS

B3082 TO BLANDFORD.

TRACK

S.V. WAY

OUTFALL

STILE

PATH.

LARGE WILLOW

RIVER STOUR

STILE AND BRIDGE

10

STILE AND BRIDGE

31

PART TWO - THE SPREADEAGLE SAUNTER

INTRODUCTION

With the buzz of single-engined aeroplanes, the twittering of skylarks and the constant bleating of sheep, the car park of Spreadeagle Hill, which stands on the airy downs of the Western end of Cranborne Chase and overlooks the Eastern edge of the Blackmore Vale, has long been a favourite spot for starting breezy walks or as a magnificent viewpoint above the River Stour plains for the less mobile.

Unfortunately, only one bus a week (No. 401) ventures near to Spreadeagle Hill and Ashmore but you can start Routes 1 and 3 from Compton Abbas by using Wilts and Dorset Bus Nos. X13, X38, 139 or Rural Bus No. 47. However, if you have access to a motorised vehicle, we will use the car park (at Reference ST886187 on O S Map No. 183) as our base for exploring the villages of East Compton and Compton Abbas, which lie below you in the sunny bowl between Compton and Fontmell Downs, and Ashmore (the highest village on Cranborne Chase), with its neolithic dew pond. The downs, forests and valleys which separate these villages from each other are filled with birds, rabbits, deer, sheep, cows - and ghosts. Well, that's not strictly true because the ghosts have, apparently, been laid - but more of that later.

As with most of the other walks in this book, I have tried to introduce alternative Routes which will enable you to plan long or short walks or to change your mind on the way round.

THE ALTERNATIVES

By starting at the car park in the mid-point of the longest walk, you can descend instantly to the Compton villages from Compton Down and amble back up Fontmell Down and then, on your return, decide whether to continue to Ashmore, Washers Pit and Fontmell Wood or to return another day for that entirely different walk.

ROUTE 1: Total distance 3.1/4 miles. This Route uses grassy paths and chalk tracks over high, breezy Compton Down and takes you down to join country lanes around the villages and churches of the Comptons. One church has been abandoned but the other, St Mary's in Compton Abbas, is well worth a visit. If you're there at the right time, you can get a cream tea in Compton Abbas - and that is your only chance to purchase refreshment on any part of the "Spreadeagle Saunter". Your return is by more grassy paths up to, and along the top of, Fontmell Down.

ROUTE 2: Total distance 5.1/4 miles. This Route takes you away from the edge of Cranborne Chase and shows you more of its hinterland with its woods and valleys. Within the first few yards, you find yourself on top of Melbury Down and then about to cross the grass air-strip of Compton Abbas Airfield. From there, you join a forest track through the ancient West Wood and, after descending to Shepherds' Bottom on farm tracks, you ascend to Ashmore. A short exploration of the village is recommended before you follow tracks to Washers Pit with its spooky goings-on. More woodland paths - just when you're feeling a little scared - lead you back, through Fontmell Wood, to cross the top road and return along a fine National Trust path.

ROUTE 3: Total distance 8.1/2 miles. Surprise, Surprise! This is just Routes 1 and 2 combined and it gives you a wonderful whole day's walking with the chance to enjoy the completely different landscapes of both Routes.

STAGE MILEAGES

STAGE	MILES	TOTAL MILES

ROUTE 1:

1	Spreadeagle Hill to East Compton	1.25	1.25
2	East Compton to Compton Abbas	.75	2
3	Compton Abbas to Spreadeagle Hill	1.25	3.25

ROUTE 2:

1	Spreadeagle Hill to Compton Abbas Airfield	1.25	1.25
4	Compton Abbas Airfield to Ashmore	1	2.25
5	Ashmore to Washers Pit	1.50	3.75
6	Washers Pit to Fontmell Hill	.75	4.50
7	Fontmell Hill to Spreadeagle Hill	.75	5.25

ROUTE 3:

1 - 3 As Route 1 (3.25 miles) and 1 - 7 As Route 2 (5.25 miles) · 8.50

ROUTE LAYOUT

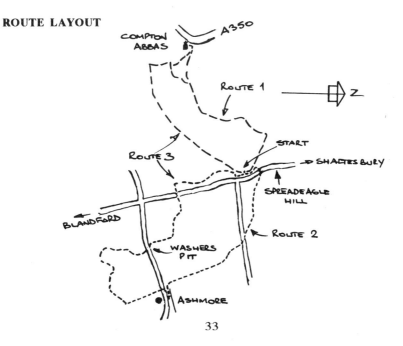

33

STAGE 1

SPREADEAGLE HILL TO EAST COMPTON or THE AIRFIELD

On arrival at the gravel parking area at the top of Spreadeagle Hill, have a long look down into the plains of the River Stour. This is a fine viewpoint at just under 750 ft above sea level and, on a clear day, you can see Hambledon Hill fort down on your left and, sweeping across the plain, Sturminster Newton and Sherborne.

Walk out of the car park and turn left along the edge of the road for 200 yards until you reach the safety of a farm track which leads instantly to a gate and a stile. *A gate in the car park leads into the tumuli field which runs alongside the road and another gate comes out into this track area but I can't recommend it as a safe alternative because it isn't a designated Footpath.* However, you're now safely on Compton Down with a wire fence on your left and a National Trust "Melbury Hill" sign on your right.

ROUTE 1:   Keep following the LH fence along the edge of the down, noticing a gate over the fence from whence emerges a farm track, until you come to a stile. Ancient cross dykes lie just to your right.   Go over the stile and walk away from the fence, up and over the saddle between Compton Down and Melbury Hill.   The viewpoint of Melbury Beacon is over on your right, at 863 ft.   Over the brow you will find the farm track which emanates from the gate that you noticed earlier.   Join this track and follow it downhill to a gate next to another National Trust "Melbury Hill" sign.   Go through the gate into a sloping field and follow the track down to the farm gate in the bottom LH corner, next to a cattle trough.   Through this gate, keep on the track, alongside the RH fence and past a gate, to a final gate which leads onto a muddy track between hedges with farm buildings and two gates on your left and a high bank on your right.   Follow the track down to a T-junction with a tarmac lane and turn left.   Now turn to Stage 2.

ROUTE 2:   After 100 yards, bear right, through some grass-covered mounds of old building remains, to a stile in the fence which brings you back out onto Spreadeagle Hill.   Over the stile, carefully cross the road to the right of two stiles in the opposite wire fence.   This one is labelled "Footpath" whilst the left one leads onto the National Trust path over "Melbury Down".   The field path along the wire fence is very long and much abbreviated on the Sketch Map so take your time and enjoy the views into the valley down on your left - noticing the deep, ancient tracks which come up from Melbury Abbas at the bottom of the hill.   When you reach a wire fence across your path, turn right and follow it uphill across the field to a gate and stile in the hedge at the top.   Climb over the stile onto the sloping approach to the landing strip.   Stop and look across the landing strip and envisage your route across it by aiming for the LH end of the dense wood on the other side.   The very long wood is darkest whilst it harbours evergreen pine trees and, near its LH end, the pines are finished and there are about three very large oaks still further left.   The official Footpath heads diagonally across the wide landing strip towards these end trees and arrives at a gate or a stile - both close together in a wooden fence.   If you are worried about crossing the strip and would like to get across more quickly, turn left and follow the hedge for about 200 yards before crossing the airfield.   If you decide on this course, go straight across the airstrip to find the gate and stile.   Either will bring you to the Footpath-arrowed stile onto the top, tarmac road.   Cross over to the entrance into "West Wood".   Go around the barrier onto the straight track which descends slightly with a row of trees and a wire fence before the field on your left and with the deep woods on your right.   Keep following the long track down and turn to Stage 4.

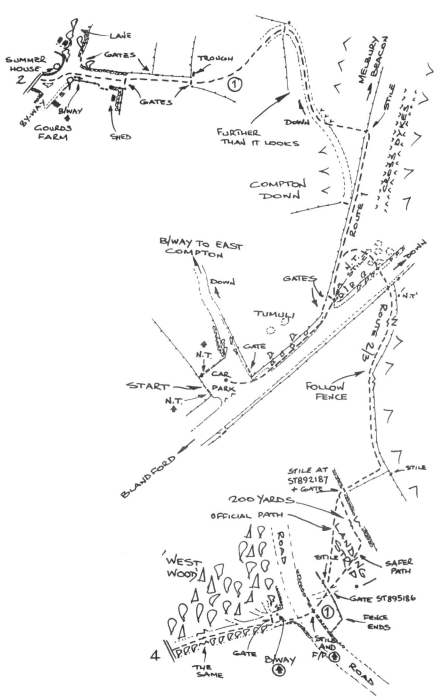

STAGE 2

EAST COMPTON TO COMPTON ABBAS

You have arrived in East Compton and you should follow the high stone wall on your right round into the lane ahead. The cottages of East Compton and Compton Abbas are almost entirely stone-built using the Shaftesbury glaucanitic sandstone. This is a porous stone which matures to a pleasant grey-green with a lovely rustic surface .

The farmhouse and buildings on your right are built opposite the remains of the original church of St Mary's, East Compton. The tower still stands defiantly above the leaning, lichen-covered gravestones in the elevated churchyard whilst, against the boundary wall, stand a stone mounting-block and a small post box.

Keep following the lane, past an abundance of stone walls and a Bridleway turning down to your left. The lane continues to harbour walls, stables, gateways to fields and cottages all along your route until, on a left bend in the lane, there is a farm gate and a Footpath-signed stile in the RH hedge. After the stile, there is a bungalow and a row of cottages with a telephone box in the verge, followed by "Lot's Cottage" - all on your left. The RH hedge is now on a high bank as the lane drops to a left turning after the entrance to a lovely garden behind the long, stone corner house.

At this T-junction, keep straight on to visit St Mary's church in Compton Abbas or turn left for the quickest way back to Fontmell Down. It's only 200 yards to the church and it's not much out of the way so I'll assume that you're all going straight on. Uphill now, with banked hedges either side, keep going until you pass the old chapel on your left and a fine stone cottage on the next LH corner. The long stone cottage on the opposite RH corner is "The Old Forge". Go past the LH turning for now, and go up the steps in the LH embankment into a small wood which adjoins the very busy A350 bottom road from Shaftesbury to Blandford.

Follow the path through the woods and down a single step onto the lawn of the Compton Abbas School, past a bench and the swings. Quietly pass the school building and keep close to the iron fence on your way to the steps and gate which lead you into the barrier-protected area next to the A350. There is another bench, commemorating the Coronation of Queen Elizabeth 2nd, in this stone wall so you may be permitted a short break. There are bus stops for Shaftesbury and Blandford here. Also a telephone box and a post box so communication with the outside world is relatively easy from here. If you feel like a cream tea, there is a Tea Room just down the road in the Blandford direction - but mind the traffic.

Compton, meaning "farm in the valley", comes from 'cumb' and 'tun'. In 955 AD, a Charter granted 10 hides of land in Compton to the Nunnery at Shaftesbury; hence the *Abbas* connection. The first church, of indeterminate date, was pulled down and some of the stones were used in the foundations of this 1867 church of St Mary. It has a Norman font and a chalice of 1665 - the "Cumpton Abbies Cup" so it clearly has a history. It's a pity there are no guides available.

Now, back outside, return through the school grounds and out into the lane opposite The Old Forge (B & B at the time of writing). Turn right at the foot of the steps and right again to descend the high-banked, tree and harts tongue fern-filled lane to emerge at the bottom where those who aren't visiting the church will come down the lane from your left. Turn right and follow the lane, past "Old Dairy Farm" cottage.

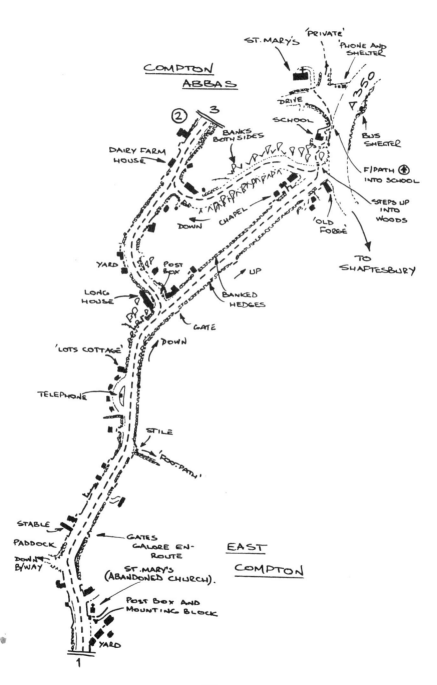

STAGE 3

COMPTON ABBAS TO SPREADEAGLE HILL

With the high bank on your right and a wooden fenced garden on your left, turn down into the grassy track with the overgrown stone wall, signposted "Gore Clump 1.1/2". After the LH paddock there is a pond which feeds a small stream running alongside this path before it disappears on your left.   There is an open bank and some trees leading around the right/left zig-zag as you pass a garden gate and a field gate on your right.   Upwards now, keep following this sunken, shady path with high fields on either side, around another right bend and down again to a half gate which brings you out into a long, downhill field.

Follow the wire fence on your right, down past a farm gate and a circular cattle trough, from where your narrow path continues uphill, past a small, banked clump of trees on your right.

Go over the unsigned stile by the next farm gate which faces you and swing round to your left, keeping close to the fences if the ground is ploughed or cropped.   Aim for the green track which goes up between the banked trees and the RH wire fence to a gate with an adjacent white arrow.

Through the gate, you will see another National Trust sign telling you that you are on the lower slopes of Fontmell Down.   Sheep and cattle tracks come in from your right and cross the slopes whilst your track leads steeply uphill past a few hawthorns and, narrowing, goes by a slumped, chalky area on the right.   The slopes drop away quite steeply to your left but this track is a fairly comfortable climb.   When you reach the RH wire fence near the top of the incline, go past the N T-arrowed stile to Fore Top and keep following the grassy track.   After the mixed wood on your right, go past another Footpath-arrowed stile and cross another dyke similar to that on Compton Down.   Now, follow the RH wire fence all the way to the N T-signed stile next to the farm gate which opens onto your starting point.

If you're only doing the shorter Route 1 today, you've arrived - but, if you're going to complete the **Route 3** "total" circuit, turn to Stage 1 again and follow the **Route 2** directions for Compton Abbas Airfield.   The Route covers a fascinating 5.1/4 miles, so you shouldn't miss it.

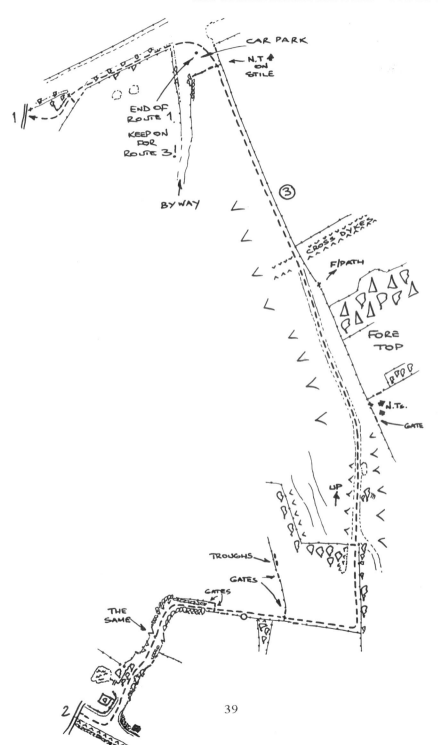

STAGE 4

COMPTON ABBAS AIRFIELD TO ASHMORE

After about 1/4 mile, you reach the end of West Wood where a very wide area, with a plethora of gates and bits of fence on your right and a gate in the LH hedge, brings you to a gate across your path.   Go through the gate and you are in a high field overlooking Shepherd's Bottom ahead of you.   Follow the green track along the LH hedge and fence, past a cattle trough and stiles in the hedge, to the next gate, before which your track divides to the right.   Go through the gate with hedges on either side and follow the track across the open field to the next gate in the wire fence.   Through this gate, the track descends more steeply, with a bank on your left and with a steep drop into Shepherd's Bottom on your right.   At the bottom of the track, another track runs away to your right, along the edge of a strip of mixed woodland.   Skirt around the LH end of the wood, with a "No Right of Way" gate on your left where a pre-enclosure map shows a shepherd's hut, and begin your ascent out of Shepherds Bottom, passing a stile into the long, narrow woods.

Through the farm gate, follow the grassy track up to the next fence with a wire fence on your left and a steep bank on your right.   Still climbing, the track fades as you approach the next gate and the field is frequently full of deep cow-prints in the soft soil.   On the LH fence, there is a notice banning all wheeled vehicles from this Bridleway.   With a row of ivy-clad trees on your right (very spooky at dusk), go through the next gate into a slightly sunken farm track with grass up the middle and with a hedge to your left and a fence to your right.   Keep to the track as it begins to level out after the gate in the hedge on your left.   With fences on both sides now, follow the track past a LH cattle trough, past all of the gates, past the "Ski-jump" or slurry-loading ramp, and over the mud-laden concrete track to exit onto the Ashmore road.   The farm on your left, together with all its barns and outbuildings, is Manor Farm.   Ashmore is along the road to your left whilst the RH direction leads straight to Washers Pit - but don't be in too much of a hurry to get there.   Ashmore is well worth a visit and there's a lovely, easy stroll off the road and through some special ancient woods if you come with me.   So, follow the stone wall-lined road towards Ashmore, past the entrance to Manor Farm on your left and the field gate on your right, and we'll go into the village first.

Ashmore, "Pool where ash-trees grow" from 'aesc' and 'mere', is the highest village on Cranborne Chase.   Listed as *Aisemare* in the Domesday Book, Ashmore's stone and flint Church of St Nicholas was built in 1423, repaired in 1692 and completely rebuilt in 1874 by Charles Edwards - destroying the best of the old church in the process.   (Incidentally, two of the churchwardens at that date were George Rabbetts and George Hare).   The cottages and houses along the road are built from a variety of brick, flint and the local greensand stone and roofed with clay tiles or thatch.

The neolithic dew pond is just around the corner, after the 1855 Methodist Chapel and the Old Parsonage.   In much simplified terms, it works by initial condensation of mist upon the specially constructed, insulated surface and thereafter by attracting moisture to the water surface, which is cooler than the surrounding atmosphere, faster than it can evaporate.   For details on how to construct one, see *"The Cranborne Chase Path"*.   It didn't even dry out during the drought of 1976 and had to be physically drained in 1994 so that the bottom could be resealed.

Turn to Stage 5 for the Bridleway that you passed on the way in and we'll be off again.

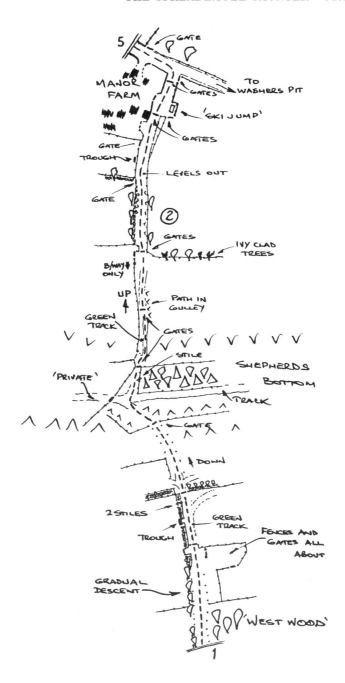

STAGE 5

ASHMORE TO WASHERS PIT

Turn left down Halfpenny Lane, the Bridleway-signed track between the LH hedge and the RH white-painted fence. Ignore the Footpath-signed stile on your left and go past the "Bridleway Only. No Motors" sign. Follow this long track between hedges at first and past a single tree on your right until it becomes wire fenced for about 1/2 mile. The Sketch Map has reduced the length of this track but it's quite a long way, past several gates, another Bridleway arrow and a "Wessex Ridgeway" arrow, before you reach your turning off. When you find another Bridleway arrow on a post on the left, turn right onto the chalk track which runs alongside a field-dividing wire fence.

This is a Footpath but the sign appears to have gone missing. However, follow the track down to a gate which leads into a fascinating wood known as Great Morris Close. This vast wood consists, unusually, of acres of coppiced hazel with ancient oaks scattered about, together with beech and pine trees. These coppiced hazels were used mainly for the fencing and pens for the vast amount of sheep in this area. The mixed wood is filled with bird song, the argumentative cackling of crows and rooks, the screeches of pheasant and the overhead mewing of buzzards. Follow the track to a junction of tracks and turn right. Ignore the track which turns off instantly left. Your track drops down and passes a peaty, hoofprint-filled track on the right at the bottom of the dip. Keep on up the gravel and grass track with dense coppiced hazel on your right and thinner coppicing on your left, past a LH grass track on a bend in your track and past two opposing faint grass tracks a little further on. Still with coppice on either side and a few ancient scattered oak trees, the main track bends very sharply right (at * on the Map) to a broken, old wooden shed next to a gate which leads into a field and the exit from the hoofprint-filled track which you saw beginning earlier in the bottom of the dip.

If you go that way, turn left at the wooden shed and keep to the main track which then turns around a left bend and continues straight for about 1/4 mile between a deep coppice wood on your left and coppice and a wire fence on your right.

However, to keep you out of the hoof holes for a while longer, turn left at junction * on the Map instead. This is much softer and more gentle on the ankles as it wends its way between older coppiced hazels until it reaches a T-junction. Turn very sharply right, almost as if doubling back, and you will rejoin the main track at a fork. Turn very sharply left and follow the hoof-holed track past a partially cleared area on your left and on between more coppiced hazels but, this time, with a fenced field on your right. At the end of this track, where a wider but less distinct track goes off to your left between ancient scattered oaks, the field ends on your right and the track goes straight on - grassier now - into a mixed beech and pine wood.

Follow this grassy track to another T-junction and turn sharp right to pass between a phalanx of tall pine trees guarding the track. The trees have been harvested and are more thinly spaced here as you begin a slight descent. The track bends right as a more grassy track goes off to your left at a Bridleway-arrowed post. Follow the main track, passing a Footpath-arrowed gate which leads back towards Ashmore, wending down between a RH fenced field and a LH sloping beech and pine wood, to emerge, past a Forestry Commission barrier and a Bridleway arrow, onto the Ashmore road. Turn left into the open Stubhampton Bottom entrance at Washers Pit and have a look at the Stage 6 text before you head on up the road - but don't linger too long.

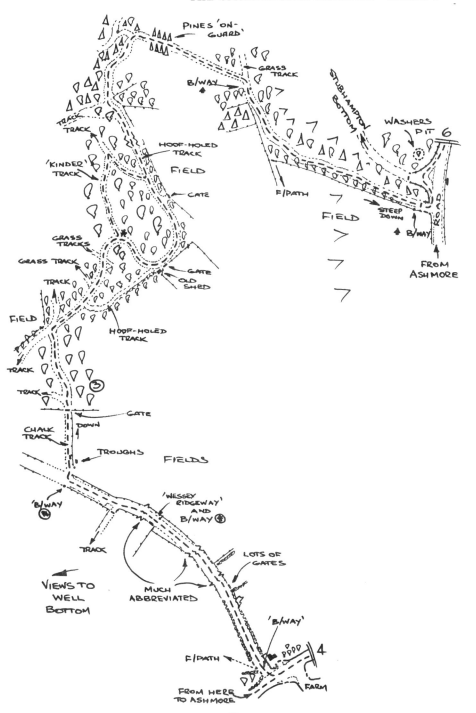

43

WASHERS PIT TO FONTMELL HILL

Strung out along this valley, there are several ancient, disused limepits which were once used for burning hair from hides of cattle and sheep.   Washers Pit stands in line with these and the only weird tales in the Ashmore area are connected with this spot - O S Map Reference ST897168 (L V Grinsell's Barrow 3e).   Let me quote from E W Watson's "History of the Parish of Ashmore 1651-1820" (dated 1890)   I wouldn't expect you to believe anything which isn't authenticated.   "There was another barrow, over which the road to Fontmel now runs, by Folly Hanging Gate, near Washers Pit.   In this lonely place, till within living memory, strange sounds were made by creatures in the air called Gappergennies, or however the name may be spelt. When, perhaps 50 years ago, a metalled road was made to Fontmel instead of the old cart-track, this barrow, which lay close to the old road and on the line of the new one, was dug up, and the bones it contained buried in the churchyard....since then, the strange sounds have not been heard".

At this spot, a woman was found hanging by her hair from a tree overhanging the now-vanished well.   She was cut down by a serving woman who was moved to visit the spot by three successive dreams.   If she had responded after the first or second dream, I wonder if she'd have been too early.   And before you go - a woman in white is said to brush against travellers in the dark between Washers Pit and Spinneys Pond.

Now, continue up the road, past the gate into Shepherds Bottom and turn right into the Bridleway along the RH edge of Fontmell Wood, noticing the sunken track on your right which would lead straight to Washers Pit if the new road hadn't cut through it.   Follow the grassy, rutted Bridleway with beech-clad slopes and a clearing on your left and Shepherds Bottom on your right.   The track bends as it begins a slight ascent with scots pines, oaks and coppiced hazel and, approaching a mighty scots pine on a RH bend, you will see the ancient track in the coppice on your right.   At the next clearing, a steep track turns left up the hillside just before a deer fence-enclosed area with a blue, straight-on arrow painted on the corner beech tree.

Turn left up the hill track with the beech wood on your left and a row of beeches on your right against the deer fence.   As a grass track goes off left, the fenced enclosure finishes as well and, a few yards further on, another track goes down to your right and you join the main track coming from your left.   Keep following the straight-on direction, past another blue arrow on a corner beech and an avenue of lofty scots pines along the next left, wide track.   Still keep straight on, not so steep now, but still ascending with the skyline showing through the beech wood on your left and with thinner trees on the right slopes.

Another track turns off right, at the start of a bank and gulley alongside your track on the right with a deciduous pine wood behind it.   Overgrown dyke, ancient track, deer defence bank or what?   Your guess is as good as mine.   Anyway, keep going, past another left turn and a right track beginning on the other side of the dyke.   There are now coppiced hazels on either side of the track and a field beyond the hazels on your left and, as the track widens, you go past two gates into the LH field and a World War II shelter enclosed on your left amid some scots pines and straggly beeches.   Now, after tracks to left and right, you arrive at 1.1/2 steel gates which bring you out onto the top Blandford to Shaftesbury road.   Go through the smaller gate and carefully cross the road to the Footpath- arrowed stile next to the gate in the opposite fence.

BLANDFORD

NEW TREES

7

DOWN

F/PATH ON STILE

WW2

TRACK

GATES

SHAFTESBURY

GATES

TRACK

GATES

FIELD

DARK WOOD

AVENUE

B/WAY

DEAD-END TRACK

DYKE, TRACK OR BANK?

TRACKS

TRACK

TRACKS

UP

DEER FENCES

B/WAY

TRACK

SHEPHERD'S BOTTOM

FONTMELL WOODS

CLEARING

CLEARING

OLD TRACK OR STREAM?

"B/WAY BLANDFORD/ SHAFTESBURY ROAD 1"

5

FONTMELL HILL TO SPREADEAGLE HILL

Safely over the wooden stile, you will find a new wood on your left with older pine trees beyond them.   There is a sloping field on your right, probably sheep-filled, and with a fine view over it to Melbury Beacon over the top of Fontmell Down.   Follow the grass track away from the road and, as you descend, the path narrows and runs along the top of a ridge, bending around some older beeches between you and the field.   Now, go down to the stile in the fence facing you.   The track which runs downhill on the other side would take you to Fontmell Magna and you are invited that way by a painted Footpath arrow on a beech tree.   Our route is the main, straight track which comes from the LH field gate and extends far to your right in a straight line.   From this stile, you can see the Iron age hill fort of Hambledon Hill - more of which later.   For now, turn right, with the field on your right and with the beech-clad slopes above Longcombe Bottom on your left.   Follow this track for a good 500 yards and you will arrive at a 1/2 gate into the RH field and a stile next to a gate across your path.   Notices advise you that you are entering the "Dorset Wildlife Trust Nature Reserve", management of which is "...Grant Aided by English Nature".

Over this stile, another gate leads into the RH, high field and you then drop down as the track turns sharply round to the left en route for Longcombe Bottom.   Don't follow it!   Keep following the fenced field on your right by going up a steep bank, on a narrower path behind scrubby hawthorn bushes.   Between the bushes, there are delightful views into the glorious, narrow-bottomed, steep-sided valley of Longcombe Bottom, beyond the valley to Hambledon Hill and across the valley to Fore Top and its cross-dykes.   These were probably more to stop cattle from wandering too far from the upper slopes than for defensive purposes.

Anyway, enjoying the views on the last 1/2 mile of this lovely walk, keep on the narrow path until you reach a cattle trough.   From here, turn slightly down the slope towards a stile and gate in the facing wire fence.   The sign confirms that you are in the "Fontmell Down Nature Reserve" but, still admiring the lovely view, cross the top field towards the LH corner of the small, fenced pine wood.

Turning right around the wood's far side, walk up towards the grassy banks facing you, past the fenced turning between the two small woods.   Follow the next fence round to the "Fontmell and Melbury Estates" notice and then head up to the far, top LH corner of the field where you will find a "National Trust Path" stile in the wire fence.   The road opposite follows the old Ridgeway which you crossed after the Airfield on your way into West Wood.

Over the stile, follow the LH fence along the edge of the road for 1/4 mile back to the car park where you started.   Before you go home, let me tell you about a link between Compton Abbas below you and Hambledon Hill.   During the Civil War, several of the local Royalist leaders were seized by Colonel Fleetwood during a secret meeting in Shaftesbury on August 2nd 1645.   Mr Bravel, the rector of St Mary's in Compton Abbas, was Commander of the Dorset Clubmen who met up on Hambledon Hill two days later to march on Shaftesbury to rescue them.   But Cromwell was already on his way to Shaftesbury with 1000 dragoons.   In the ensuing hour-long battle on Hambledon Hill, with between 2500 and 4000 Clubmen, 60 Clubmen were killed, 400 were taken prisoner (including 4 rectors and curates and 200 wounded) whilst the rest escaped to fight another day.   Of Cromwell's men, 13 were killed

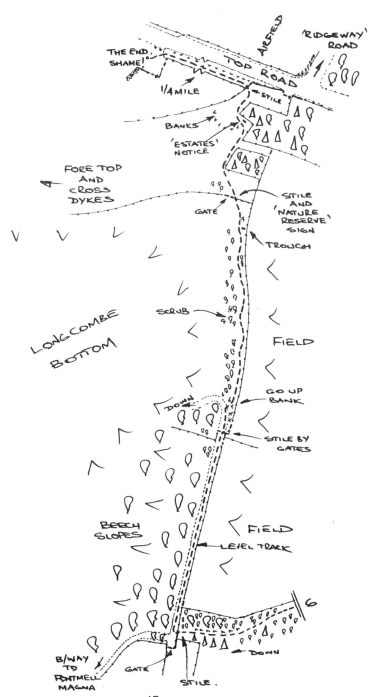

THE END
SHAME!

1/4 MILE

'RIDGEWAY'
ROAD

AIRFIELD

TOP ROAD

STILE

BANKS

'ESTATES'
NOTICE

FORE TOP
AND
CROSS
DYKES

STILE
AND
'NATURE
RESERVE'
SIGN

GATE

TROUGH

LONGCOMBE
BOTTOM

SCRUB

FIELD

DOWN

GO UP
BANK

STILE BY
GATES

BEECH
SLOPES

FIELD

LEVEL TRACK

B/WAY
TO
FONTMELL
MAGNA

GATE

STILE.

DOWN

47

PART THREE - THE STOUR VALLEY STROLL

Roll on, fair Stour! As through the fields you stray,
The Miller drains your flow to drive his wheel.
One moment lingering on your winding way,
Short gossip have with mill, then onward steal.

John Gibson, Stour Provost

INTRODUCTION

"The Stour Valley Path" was the first of my published long-distance Dorset walks books and, as such, it holds a special affection for me.   Notwithstanding this, I only decided to go into print in the first place in order to share the experience of walking the length of the River Stour with as many fellow walkers and lovers of the Dorset countryside as possible.   In this day walk presented here, the stages from Marnhull to Fifehead Magdalen and Stour Provost are very little changed from those same stages in *"The Stour Valley Path"* but some new stiles have been reintroduced in a couple of places where the official Footpath had been previously obliterated.   I have added the section back from Stour Provost to Marnhull to form a complete circuit with a lovely, easy stroll over riverside farmland.   The route includes a restored mill and its associated ponds, the chance to visit two superb little churches and the opportunity for me to repeat a few scary tales which are associated with this part of Dorset.   This is not a long walk and allows plenty of time for reading inscriptions during your church visits and to linger by the side of the River on your way.

Access to Marnhull isn't a problem.   There are Wilts and Dorset services Nos. 117 and 190 and Rural Services Nos. 15, 36, 50 and 109.   Free Car Parking is available in the Car Park in Burton Street by the Surgery.   The starting point for this stroll is at Map Reference ST 775193 on O S Map No. 183, outside the Post Office in Burton Street, immediately opposite Sackmore Lane.

ROUTE LAYOUT

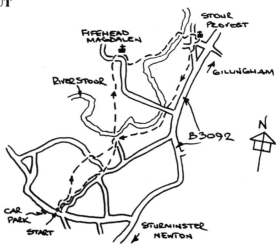

48

STAGE MILEAGES

STAGE	MILES	TOTAL MILES
1 Marnhull to Fifehead Magdalen	1.50	1.50
2 Fifehead Magdalen to Stour Provost	1	2.50
3 Stour Provost to Marnhull	1.75	4.25

In the Rev. John Hutchins "History and Antiquities of the County of Dorset" we find that Marnhull stands "surrounded nearly on three sides by the River Stour which rises from seven wells or springs at what is commonly known as Stourton in Wiltshire but the proper name is StourFont or StourHead". Marnhull gets its name from "Marl Hill, a hill of marle as the soil is chiefly a white marl or clay, which hardens in air to freestone, easily worked when first dug but gets hard by time".

The parish church is St Gregory's which you will need to detour about 1/2 mile to see - by following Burton Street out of town into Church Hill. It has an elegant, lofty tower of the 15th Century which is visible for miles in this pastoral landscape. Inside, in the North arcade, is a remnant of the 12thC building in a single carved capital whilst the 15thC nave roof and alabaster figures are particularly fine.

Whilst on the subject of that part of Marnhull, let me tell you a tale of witches which is repeated in a similar vein in many villages in the West. Our story concerns one Mrs Fudge who lived in Marnhull around the end of the reign of Queen Victoria. She lived in a cottage at the lower end of Church Hill, just down the road from St Gregory's and, as she stood by her front door one day, she saw a hag-like woman coming down the hill towards her. Unfortunately, Mrs Fudge had the temerity to laugh at the sight of this strange woman and the hag observed her amusement. That night, in bed, Mrs Fudge felt a weight upon her legs which moved slowly up her body to her chest. She screamed out in horror and her son burst into her room. As soon as the door opened, the heavy lump fell off and Mrs Fudge distinctly heard the hag walk down the stairs and out of the door. Even now, there is an expression used in this area for anyone who has a nightmare. They are said to have been "hag-ridden".

Now, before you start, I'll tell you why the corner of Sackmore Lane is particularly chosen as a starting point. At nearby Todber, locally said to be named from "trod bare" by troops at some great un-named battle, a great number of human remains were found during marl quarrying in 1870-71, although it is also possible that this was a plague burial ground. At midnight on a certain date, a ghostly funeral was seen crossing Sackmore Lane from Fillymead (the old village green) to Dunfords. No mourners attended this funeral and even the faces of the bearers were hidden beneath a pall which covered the coffin. The same tale is told of Grove Field, near Nash Court which is practically on the same line from Fillymead to Todber. You will be pleased to hear that you'll be passing Nash Court on your return as well. Better move on now before you get too cold and - "Try to get back before midnight!"

STAGE 1

MARNHULL TO FIFEHEAD MAGDALEN

Facing the Post Office in Burton Street, with Sackmore Lane behind you, turn right along Burton Street as far as Love Lane.   Opposite the sturdy, stone porch of Banbury House turn left down Love Lane and follow it, past a few houses on left and right, to the first bend where you will find a steel stile next to a farm gate on the bank.   Over the Footpath-arrowed stile, go straight across the field to another stile by the gate in the opposite hedge.   Follow the direction of the arrow on the stile across the next field, just to the left of the LH of the three big oaks in the middle of the field.   This will bring you to a new stile in what appears to be somebody's back garden.   It is actually a Public Footpath which has existed for many years but nearly went missing until *"The Stour Valley Path"* exposed it.   Over this stile with the Footpath arrow, follow the path around the bends, over the next two stiles and down the wooden steps onto Haims Lane.   Turn immediately right and then take the next arrowed stile in the LH hedge opposite "Haims".

Over this stile, aim diagonally right towards the electricity pole which is lurking in the hedge near the far RH end of the field. You will find a pair of stiles about 50 yards beyond this pole, one either side of a particularly wide, embankment-covering hedge. Over the second stile, bear left across the near corner of the next field to a pair of old oaks next to another arrowed stile by a steel farm gate.   This leads you out onto a lane opposite a three-storeyed stone house and the "Catholic Church of Our Lady". Turn left and follow the lane, past the fenced LH field and Meadow Cottage on your right, to the end.   There are gates all around and signposts pointing to "Fifehead Magdalen 1" and "Stour Provost 1.1/4".

Go through the pair of gates onto the gravel driveway of Withy Cottage and No. 2, as this is the Public Footpath, and quietly follow the RH, hedged stone wall to the next stile which leads you into a small field/old orchard.   Keep to the RH hedge and fence to reach the cattle barriers which guard the concrete bridge across our first meeting with the River Stour.   Over the bridge, follow the faint path, to the left of the electric wires' support post, to the LH end of the hedge facing you.   On arrival at the hedge corner, bear slightly right and aim for the farthest end of this very long field - the gate you will eventually need is 100 yards left of the far end of this hedge.

Through this gate, turn instantly right and follow the cut grass path next to the hedge around a left bend to lead you uphill with a ditch between you and the hedge.   At the top, you will find a tarmac track across your path.   Turn right onto the track and go through the gateway.   Immediately turn left and follow the edge of this field around the border of a small copse, keeping to the LH grassy bank.   In a few yards, the bank turns right and you then you come to a gap in the bank.   Turn left through some broken gateposts into the next field.   Follow the grassy path alongside the RH hedge, past an opening and up to the top RH corner where a stile with a fingerpost leads you into a narrow, hedged hollow-way which comes out next to the Old School, Fifehead Magdalen.   Cross over to the pavement on the Old Post Office side, turn right and follow the road, past stone cottages on your left, to a paddock at the end where a drive goes to the left and a narrow path, to the left of the high stone wall with the two iron gates facing you, leads to The Church of St Mary Magdalene.

Now that you're here, turn to Stage 2 where there is more space to tell you about this lovely church.

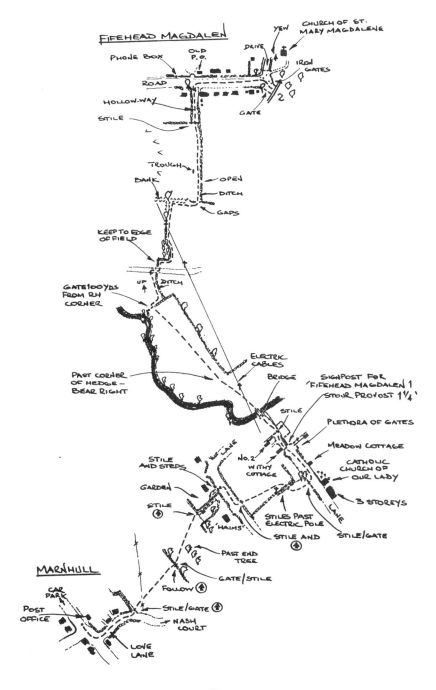

FIFEHEAD MAGDALEN TO STOUR PROVOST

The Church of St Mary Magdalene gives Fifehead Magdalen the second part of its name - the first deriving from its old measurement of "five hides of land"- whilst, in the Domesday Book as *Fifhide*, it boasted two mills and was held by Earl Hugh. The lovely church has been much rebuilt over the years but it has escaped the excesses of the Victorian era. Its bright interior contains a magnificent 18thC memorial to Sir Richard Newman, who died in 1721, his two wives and three daughters. Outside, under the great yew tree, have a look at the tomb of Thos. Newman who died in 1688. Now - did the well-known homily about swallows and spring (or summer) inspire this inscription or was this verse the original?

> *Whilst Tower remaine, or spring my yew,*
> *Here I shall lie as green, young, new,*
> *.......news to us good times shall bring,*
> *One swallow doth not make the spring.*

Back outside the churchyard, past the iron gates, turn down the lane and go past the stile and gate on the LH bend which share a sign "West Stour. Keep to the Footpath". Keep on down for about 100 yards to the next LH farm gate in the hedge. Here, the sign proclaims "Footpath. Stour Provost 1/2". Through the gate, keep to the LH hedge as the field drops down to a LH arrowed stile, . Go over the stile and you will find yourself in a high field with marsh grass growing abundantly near the top. Looking down the field, aim for the stile in the fence at the bottom near to the closest bend in the River Stour. Down at the arrowed stile in a section of wooden fence, turn right and follow the edge of the Stour all the way to the next footbridge. Towards the end of this fine, riverside stroll, there are some lovely views of the sluice gates and pool of Stour Provost Mill on the other side. Go past the "Private Fishing" sign and the arrowed post by the gate and cross the bridge.

On the other side, between two branches of the Stour, turn right to the next gate onto the path over the sluice gates where you now pass through private land. Before you go through the next gate - the plaque on the mill wall commemorates the partial restoration of the mill, after more than 60 years disuse, by Derek Llewelyn who used it to generate electricity. Here, I would like to thank John Gibson, ex-resident of Stour Provost who allowed me to use a part of his poem, which was inspired by his friend's restoration of the mill, in the Introduction to "The Stour Valley Stroll".

Now, after this gate, go through the wicket gate on your immediate left which brings you out on the other side of the second tributary. Cross the 'garden' lawn to a stile in the wire fence and go over into the steeply sloping field. Head diagonally right up this field to the top by a low stone barn. Go over the stile by the gate and follow the wide, grassy track with various stone walls on either side. Bearing right, the track becomes tarmac and emerges onto a T-junction. Turn right and stroll up into Stour Provost. The path on your left, between the first stone cottages, leads to the lovely early 14th and 15thC church of St Michael which was restored in 1838. It has a fine, big lych gate and an avenue of pollarded trees leading to the front porch. It has a lovely chancel ceiling, elegant lancet windows on the South side and a "striking clock with no face" which was built by William Monk of Berwick St John in 1735. After your visit, return to the road and continue through the village. Leave by keeping straight on at the crossroads, past the thatched cottage on the RH corner, and climb over the first stile in the wire fence of the field on your right. Turn left to the next stile by the gate into the next field and climb over into a second field.

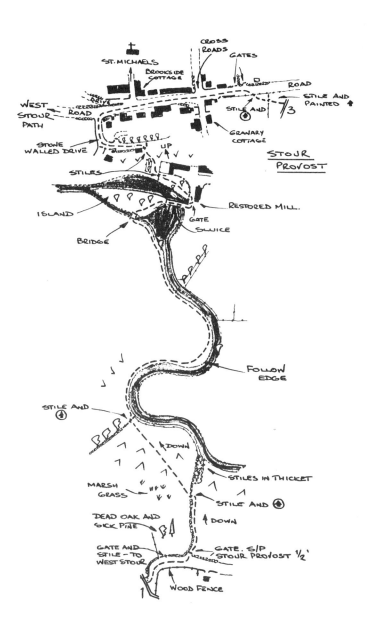

STAGE 3

STOUR PROVOST TO MARNHULL

Most of Stour Provost was owned by the Provost and scholars of Kings College, Cambridge from about 1450 to 1925. It had been owned before then by the French monastery of Priaulx but, during a dispute with France, Stour Provost was seized and given as an endowment to Kings College. During the enclosures of 1624, a Chancery decree maintained that the villages "1300 acres of large pasture ground or waste...is used to small profit. By division and enclosure it would yield much greater profit to all tenants *and also to the Provost, fellows and scholars at Kings College"*.

Right. You can go now. Keep straight on past the fenced barn and over the pair of stiles on either side of the deep hedge. In this next field, go past the RH end of the fenced enclosure to find another pair of stiles, on the same line, in the opposite hedge. Over these stiles, the next field has a wire fence on your left. Follow this fence to the gate into the LH field and a trough at the end of the hedge. Go through the second gate into the next, small field - changed "by division and enclosure".

Head for the stile in the far corner, against the RH hedge, and halt awhile. This is a particularly wide field and the exit stile from it is positioned about 100 yards down to the right from the clear, farm gate opening which you can see in the hedge on the other side. The Footpath should head across the field towards the stile so, if the field isn't planted, head straight for it. However, if crops are growing and the path hasn't been cleared, it might be easier to follow the hedge all the way round anti-clockwise and approach the stile from the lower, nearer edge of the field by Trill Bridge.

Go over the stile and cross the lane to the stile in the opposite hedge. There are a couple of ponds in this field so go round the right of the smaller one to an opening in the scrubby hedge and a stile on the other side. Go straight across the rising field for a few yards and then bear slightly right towards the far gate with two Footpath arrows on the gatepost. Follow the direction along the top of a bank, with the Stour down on your right, to the next stile in the wire fence. Over this stile, keep fairly close to the LH fence and hedge to cross the brow of the sloping field and continue down the other side to the stile in the wire fence, just past a small stone shed on the LH side.

Over the stile, turn down to rejoin the lane where you entered the drive of Withy Cottage. Turn left along the lane and climb over the stile just past the Catholic Church. This time, take the left of the two Footpath options, crossing the field diagonally with Nash Court ahead of you. When you reach the far, top end by the exit gate, go over the stile in the corner into "Haims Lane" and, on the island in the T-junction, you will see a signpost which points to "Todber" to your left (That's right - of ghostly cortege fame). Follow the lane up in the "Marnhull Church" direction, past "Nash Villa" to "Nash Court Farmhouse" on the RH corner. The fine, stone building behind the boundary wall on the opposite corner is the 1834 Nash Court as the original 15thC building was demolished in 1831. Turn right up "Love Lane" and immediately climb over the stile on your right onto a safer path which follows the high-banked lane. Keep to this path, over the first stile and return into Love Lane either by the first arrowed stile after the farm gate on your left or by the second un-arrowed stile. Once back into the lane, follow it between the high-banked fields, past one last farm gate and one last stile on your right, to where you left Love Lane to begin "The Stour Valley Stroll" a few hours earlier. Well, that's the end, so walk back into Marnhull and enjoy your memories of a fine ramble.

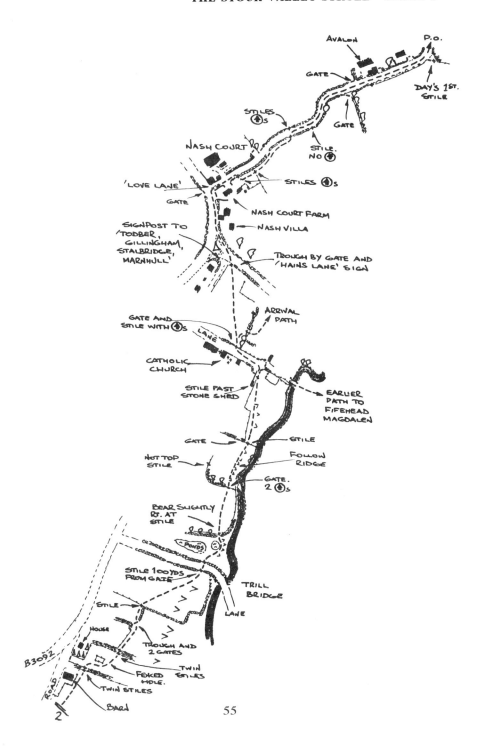

PART FOUR - THE ABBOTSBURY AMBLE

INTRODUCTION

First of all, let me dispel the title's allusion to an 'amble'. It's just that I couldn't find another expression meaning "a walk" which begins with an A. This walk needs strong legs and proper hiking boots. For most walks in the countryside, I would never be happy in anything less than proper hiking boots although many people seem to manage quite well with trainers or wellingtons - but there are steep hills on this walk whilst, in the winter or any rainy season, some of the tracks can be quite muddy. In particular, the descent from Abbotsbury Castle to East Bexington Farm is deep, steep and notoriously slippery - except in times of drought when it is just steep and rough on the ankles.

Over the last thousand years, Abbotsbury has only had two owners. First there was the Abbey and then the Fox-Strangways family, the Earls of Ilchester. The Swannery has been maintained by the Strangways since the Dissolution of the Monasteries by Henry VIII. The 14thC St Nicholas' church, with its 15thC tower, stands close to the remnants of the Benedictine Abbey. The church was extensively rebuilt about the end of the 15thC whilst the chancel has a plastered barrel ceiling dated 1638. There is an effigy of a 12thC abbot in the porch and the Jacobean pulpit bears pistol-shot holes dating back to the Roundheads and the Cavaliers.

St Catherine's Chapel stands, massive and conspicuous as a daytime guide to sailors and, when it was first built in 1370, it sometimes showed a beacon in times of storm .

Whether you come to Abbotsbury by car, bus or bicycle, the walks start opposite the "Ilchester Arms" in Market Street (Reference SY576853 on O S Map No. 194), near the bus stop and not far from the car park which is next to "The Swan" on the B3157 Eastbound. Several well-timed buses run to Abbotsbury. These are Southern National No. 210 from Bridport and Weymouth plus Rural Buses Nos. 61 from Wyke Regis and Dorchester and 60 from Weymouth and Bridport.

THE ALTERNATIVES

Although several circular routes of varying lengths can be chosen as you circumnavigate Abbotsbury, I have detailed just two whilst pointing out several other, un-numbered and shorter alternatives as you progress around the long Route 1. All chosen Routes begin and end in the open area outside the Ilchester Arms because it is convenient for bus stops and the car park.

ROUTE 1: Total distance 8.1/4 miles. This Route uses grassy paths and chalk tracks over high, breezy downs with great views of Chesil Beach and the sea but, when you have seen the view from the top of Abbotsbury Plains, it goes inland to visit the prehistoric Grey Mare and Her Colts and the valley farm of Gorwell. It then returns to the ridge above Abbotsbury and follows the inland "Dorset Coast Path" for a while until you reach Abbotsbury Castle hill fort. Then, the Route turns down the National Trust's steep Turks Hill to the unique natural structure of Chesil Beach and thence to the 14thC St Catherine's chapel before descending once more into the heart of Abbotsbury.

ROUTE 2: Total distance miles 3.75 miles.   After Gorwell Farm and on attaining the heights of Wear Hill, this Route turns down to Blind Lane, a grassy, gulleyed track which then passes outcrops of sandstone and a small cliff of Abbotsbury iron ore.   From there, the path continues to descend until it returns you into the village about 100 yards from where you started.

STAGE MILEAGES

STAGE	MILES	TOTAL MILES
ROUTE 1:		
1 Abbotsbury to White Hill	1	1
2 White Hill to Gorwell Farm	1	2
3 Gorwell Farm to Wears Hill	1.25	3.25
4 Wears Hill to Turks Hill	1	4.25
5 Turks Hill to Coastguard Lookout	1.75	6
6 Coastguard Lookout to St Catherine's Hill	1.25	7.25
7 St Catherine's Hill to Abbotsbury	1	8.25
ROUTE 2:		
1 - 3 Abbotsbury to Wears Hill as Route 1 to Abbotsbury turn-off	3	3
3a Wears Hill to Abbotsbury	.75	3.75

ROUTE LAYOUT

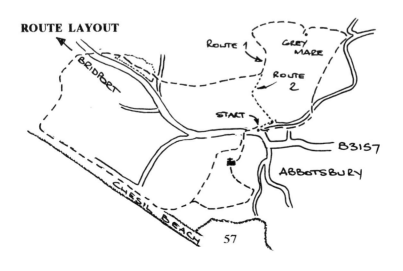

57

STAGE 1

ABBOTSBURY TO WHITE HILL

Having made your way from the bus stop or the car park to the corner of Back Lane, opposite the "Ilchester Arms", turn up Back Lane past Strangways Hall and the Old School Tea Rooms.   Continue past the 'phone box and the conveniences on the left and a ditch and hedge on the RH side.   After the old chapel and some stone cottages, the first left turn is a Bridleway down which any short-cutters will return later on Route 2.   For now, continue up the lane, past "Spring Cottage" and "The Keep" on the left and some new stone houses on the right.   With a gate leading to farm sheds on the left, the RH lane leads back down to the Abbotsbury car park and there is a banked and fenced field on the LH side of the road.   Still going uphill, after houses on the RH side and past Bishops Close, an overgrown hollow-way goes off to the left.   Just after that, you can accelerate to over 30 mph if you so wish.

The road bends left as a farm track bears off between gated hedges - still uphill and with low fields on your right.   After another 200 yards, the road bends right towards a mixed wood but you turn off here, at a Bridleway-signed gate, into a deep, steep, grassy track which begins to climb up fields on the side of White Hill.   Following the wire fence on your left, the track bends towards another gate next to a cattle trough in the facing fence.   Go through this gate into the next steep field, still on the grassy track in well-worn gulleys.   Take your time going through the gates and you can get your breath back whilst admiring the wonderful views behind you which stretch along Chesil Beach to Portland.   Higher up, you will be able to see all the way to Devon if it's a clear day.

On the way up, slumped patches of hillside show the chalk which keeps this upland area relatively dry underfoot even in rain-sodden weather.   At the top of this field, go through the half-gate on to the slopes of White Hill with a grass track coming from your left.   The Bridleway signpost just along the fence on your right points straight up the slope for "Hardy Monument" and right, along the fence, for "Lime Kiln Car Park".   Keep straight on up the hillside, aiming for the top grassy gulley.   Our route rejoins the road in a while. Clearly horses and carts (and hikers) can negotiate steeper slopes than cars because shallower slopes and a couple of bends had to be included when the tarmac road was built.

The Hardy Monument, which is the huge stone tower which you can see from the top of this hill, is commemorating the life of Thomas Masterman Hardy, Lord Nelson's flag captain at the Battle of Trafalgar who lived at Portesham, just two miles East of Abbotsbury.   This tower is visible for miles around and can be seen almost as soon as you enter Dorset from the Lyme Regis direction in the West or from the Yeovil direction in the North West.

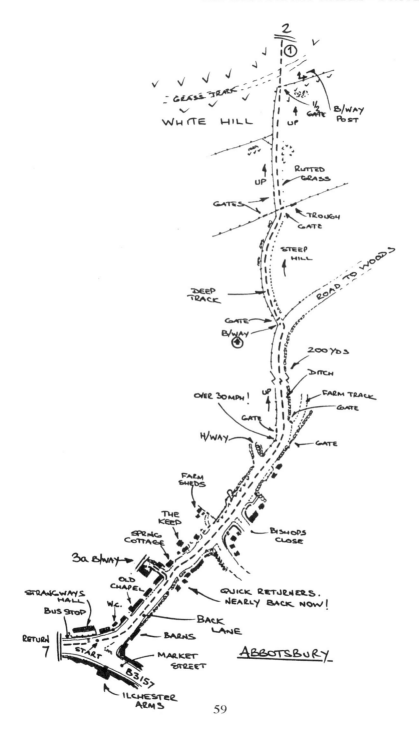

STAGE 2

WHITE HILL TO GORWELL FARM

Still upwards, follow the green track into a deep gulley between banks and lynchets and past a few hawthorn bushes on the left bank.   As a grass track comes from your left, the trail becomes clearer and firmer with chalk and flints in the track.   Go through the Bridleway-arrowed gate onto a less clear, but smooth and level, grassy track but, when it bends right towards a gate in a wire fence, keep straight on to pass the LH corner of the fenced field, next to a three-way Bridleway signpost.   You are now on the top of the ridge with the inland route of the Dorset Coast Path leading to "West Bexington 3.1/2" on the left whilst your path points, for now, to "Hardy Monument 2".   The views across a patchwork of fields to Portland are excellent.

The cleared Bridleway, which follows the RH fence and the sparse hedge on an ancient parish boundary bank, leads you down to a cattle-sorting pen which lies in the sunken track but go past the LH edge of the pen to find your half-gate exit onto the rejoining road from Abbotsbury.   The signpost points back for "West Bexington 3.1/2".

Out on the fenced road, follow it slightly uphill for a while, past the Bridleway turn-off along the edge of the escarpment which leads to "Hardy Monument".   After a passing place on the right, turn into the sharp hairpin turning on your left, following the wire fenced field on your left and with a banked hedge on your right.   The lane soon zig-zags right/left after a cattle grid and gate which lead to "Gorwell Farm Only - Camping and Caravan Club".   (Make a note: It may come in useful for a return visit).

For now, follow the lane to its sudden right turn and deterioration into a chalky track. Go through the half-gate next to the farm gate marked with two Bridleway arrows and a sign for "Kingston Russell Stone Circle".   There are so many circles, barrows, enclosures and earthworks around this small area - and the strange Valley of Stones between this spot and Little Bredy Farm - that it would be a wonderful place to explore more closely.   In this high, level field with rough grass in front of the LH banked hedge, follow the grass track past a "Danger. Low-Flying Aircraft" notice until you begin to descend slightly and pass through an opening in the bottom corner hedge. In about 15 yards, next to another "Kingston Russell Stone Circle" sign, go over the Footpath-arrowed stile in the LH hedge and bear right to follow the facing hedge along the top slope of a valley which begins in this field.

Go through the first gate in the LH hedge to find "The Grey Mare and Her Colts". This is a cromlech - a megalithic long barrow built from pudding-stones which are concretions of a gravel bed which cemented itself to the bed of chalk beneath. Lumps of this stone fell into the valley and were collected for cromlechs and circles such as this one, Kingston Russell's and the Nine Stones at Winterborne Abbas.

After viewing the stones, return through the nearby gate and bear left, not following the top hedge and fence but heading into the valley which will carry you down to the bottom far end of this long field.   Make sure that the solitary tree in a deep hole is up on your right as this will ensure that you are following the descending valley slope in the right direction.   Nearing the bottom, the slopes to right and left become steeper and you now come to a gate across your path.   Go through the gate between double fences onto a muddy (or rutted) track which approaches you from in front and turns to go up the RH valley slope.   Go straight on down the track, with Park Coppice on the LH slopes and a wire fence on your right, towards Gorwell Farm house ahead of you.

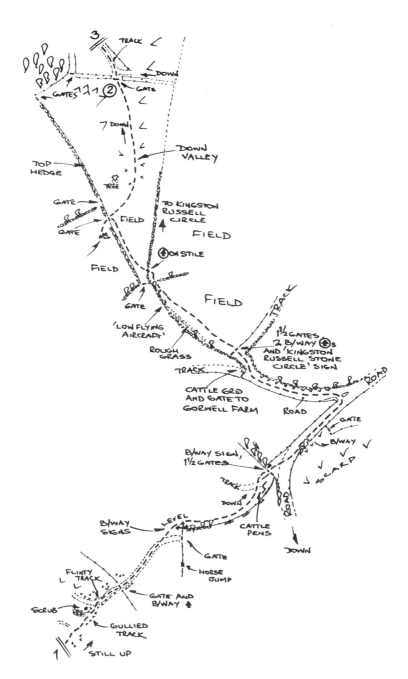

STAGE 3

GORWELL FARM TO WEAR HILL

One cold wet day, I lost a grey wool glove (left hand) somewhere here so would you please send it back to me if you find it. Keep on down the track, through a gate in the hedge across your path onto the firmer, flint and chalk track between the iron-fenced LH field (as the wooded hill comes closer) and the RH garden fence of a tree-surrounded house. At the end of the track, go through the gate into a wide open area with a paddock on the RH corner and a Bridleway/track heading off to the right to Long Bredy (no sign). The fine stone house facing you is Gorwell Farm house and it boasts a vast assemblage of assorted barns to right and left as you follow the lane up to the left between wooded slopes of beech, oak and coppiced hazel. The woods bear the names Park Coppice, Bow Coppice, Alley Moor, Bramble Coppice and Broad Coppice as you progress along the track up the valley.

A stream follows the RH edge of the track/lane, now tarmac, and you will soon see the old grass-covered dam which formed a small pond with a central island on your right. After a wide verge on your right and a small brick shed, there is also a ditch on your left as the woodland fence comes down the slope towards your lane. The lane bends left when the woods end but our route turns up the concrete track after the Bridleway-signed gate on your right. Follow the steep track between the wire fenced field and the coppice on your right. The fence ends opposite a RH gate into a hedged field but the track keeps climbing to a Bridleway-signed gate across your path. The gatepost also bears a "Macmillan Way" arrow. Go through the gate onto a high field which runs along the brow of the ridge. Keep straight on across the field on a track which is cleared of crops and drop down the other side to a collection of gates and a stile.

The LH green track, before the fence, is the Inland Dorset Coast Path route again and comes directly from where you reached White Hill on Stage 1. Go over the Footpath-arrowed stile next to the LH gate onto the slopes of Wear Hill and turn right, sparing a few moments to enjoy the views along Chesil Beach and out to sea. The path which turns left down the slope leads straight back to Abbotsbury and arrives at the 1st Bridleway after the conveniences in the village centre. This is the shorter Route 2 down. If you want to go back now on **Route 2**, turn to Stage 3a for details and the Map - but it's too nice to stop now. The ridge walk to Abbotsbury Hill Fort is superb, the stroll along the seaside is gentle and salty and St Catherine's chapel is well worth a visit, so you'll be glad you stayed.

ROUTE 1: Turn right and follow the top fence, past the Bridleway signpost confirming the ways to "Abbotsbury, Hardy Monument and Hill Fort". After the first 1/4 mile of pleasant walking along the high greensward, you pass a cattle trough and another signpost, just before you arrive at a Footpath-arrowed stile next to a gate in the hedge and fence in the top corner. Go over the stile and keep enjoying the high grass viewpoints with two barrows in the adjoining field. Note the irrigation ponds built into the levelled ground just below you. If the hillside had to be cultivated, it would have needed watering.

There are other wet areas on the slopes but these are caused by slumping (or gravity transport) - sudden, rapid soil movements caused by excessive water in the soil or clay which cause the earth to behave as a liquid and to slide down the hill. The movements are easily recognisable by the wet hollows retained behind a higher bank on the downhill front.

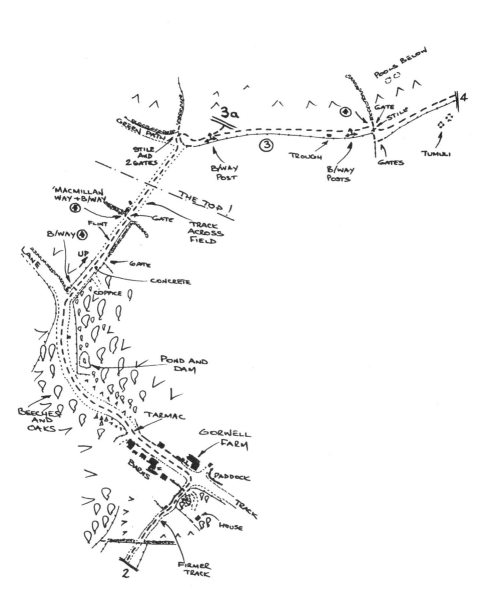

STAGE 3a

WEAR HILL TO ABBOTSBURY

ROUTE 2: This Stage is only for the short cut back to Abbotsbury.   Everybody else on the longer **Route 1** should have turned to Stage 4 by now.

It won't take long from here back to the village so, as you'll be missing the long stroll along the ridge, why not spend a few moments enjoying the fabulous views from the stone seat to the right of your descending grass track?

Over on your left, you can see the Isle of Portland extending out into the sea.   Long famous for its fine stone quarries which have provided much of the stone for buildings in London and other major cities, Portland also provided harbour facilities and a helicopter base for the Navy until it was closed down in 1995/96.   It is sad that this lively adjunct to the Dorset coastal scene is no more and the skies are no longer filled with the buzz of oversized dragonflies.   Chesil Beach, the unique bank of shingle which stretches for some 16 miles from beyond West Bay to Portland, gradually increases in height from sea level at its Western origin to Portland where it is 50 ft high.   The pebble sizes are similarly graded from pea-size at Bridport to large cobbles at the Portland end and local fishermen claim that they would be able to tell exactly where they are along the beach if they were ever shipwrecked in the dark.

Now, back to your descent.   Turn down the sunken green track, starting at the tumulus, and follow it between banks, hollows, hummocks and outcrops of greensand to a junction of green tracks next to the farm gate in the first hedge.   A signpost points back up to "Hill Fort 1.1/4" whilst the gate bears another Macmillan Way arrow.   Through the gate, follow the raised track down to another Bridleway-arrowed gate in the top corner of a wire-fenced field.   Through this gate, follow the edge of the descending low ridge straight ahead, with more stone outcrops over on your left and with a valley dropping down to your right.   Go down past a signpost which points left to "Lime Kiln Car Park" and past the banked corner of a new planting of trees on your left.   Keep to the main track now, down past a rough path which heads into the RH gorse-clad valley, following the LH bank to a gate which leads onto a narrow path in a wide gulley.

Just after the gate, you will notice that the soil and rock in the path is dark red.   This is an exposure of Abbotsbury iron ore and, after a couple of trees on your left, you will find a much-explored rock face with trees above it where geologists from miles around hope to find fossils amongst the thin beds of hematite in the oolitic, sandy deposits.   As this iron is only a thin coating on the original sand grains, there is too much silica to make the iron profitable to extract - fortunately for the conservation of the scenery hereabouts.

Follow the path down, steep but soon firmer underfoot as it widens between fenced fields.   After two opposing gates and a RH corner stile by a fine view over the village below you, follow the flinty track round to the left.   Continue down past "Copplestone", the big thatched house on the next RH bend, and past a track going up left to a paddock.   Now, with a ditch and hedge on your left, pass a thatched, stone shed and emerge out of "Blind Lane to White Hill" next to "Spring Cottage".   You're now back onto the Stage 1 map for the last few yards to the start - not that you'll need to follow it very closely.

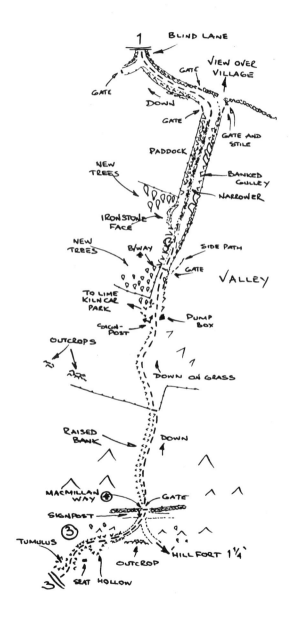

STAGE 4

WEAR HILL TO TURKS HILL

When the fenced field runs out on your right, keep straight on along the clear, wide and well-walked top route, passing another tumulus and a water tank on your right and with gorse-clad slopes on your left. You will soon see the B3157 coming up the hill on your left - a fine coast road with several viewpoints along the way. As you pass to the left of the electric cables post ahead, a Bridleway turns down to your left towards the road but keep straight on, past a LH tumulus, another electricity post, a roofless stone shed and another LH tumulus. A large farm with its own lake lies down the slopes on your right as your route follows the lower RH side of the ridge, effectively cutting off your view of the sea for a while.

The ridge is much narrower now, with scrub prevalent on both sides, and you descend into a levelled grass area with a tarmac track crossing the ridge ahead of you. Go over the Footpath-arrowed stile next to the small gate and cross the lane to the sandy lay-by opposite. Go up the sandy path in the LH end of this lay-by - up between gorse bushes - to find an Armada warning beacon next to the wire fence on the top. This beacon is part of the chain of beacons which were lit in the 1988 national celebrations of the Defeat of the Spanish Armada in 1588. If you've been on "*The Blackmore Vale Path*", you'll have seen another on top of Okeford Hill.

Zig-zag through the gorse to the Footpath-arrowed stile in the corner and climb over onto the slopes of Abbotsbury Castle. You will find yourself on the seaward side, walking in the uppermost defensive ditch. Negotiate the dyke which crosses you path and immediately turn up the steep path on your right to reach the O S plinth benchmark (set at 620 ft). From the plinth, turn left and follow the green path along the open, scrubby top of the ridge again, immediately passing another RH tumulus. Past the remains of an ancient dry-stone wall and zig-zagging down and up another crossing dyke, the path becomes gentle, downward, wide and grassy as the ridge runs out completely. Aim for the stile which you can see ahead of you in the corner, at the junction of the RH dry-stone wall and the LH road fence. The stile carries a Footpath arrow whilst the adjacent sign indicates that it is now 4.1/2 miles back to the Hardy Monument and only 1 mile ahead to West Bexington.

Very carefully cross the B3157 to the facing stile which stands at another dry-stone wall/wire fence junction where a National Trust sign informs you that you are now on the slopes of "Turks Hill". Follow the stone wall down the grassy field to the corner where a signpost confirms the West Bexington and Hardy Monument directions - but the arm which should direct you to "Chesil Beach 1" was broken off when I last came this way. Actually, it was lying on the ground and bearing a hand-written addition "Very Bad Path". Fair enough - this is where you will need your best gripping boots because the clay and chalk are particularly prone to releasing ground water onto these slopes whilst the steep hillside path is tightly contained between the stone wall and the dense gorse. So, gird up you loins and down you go!

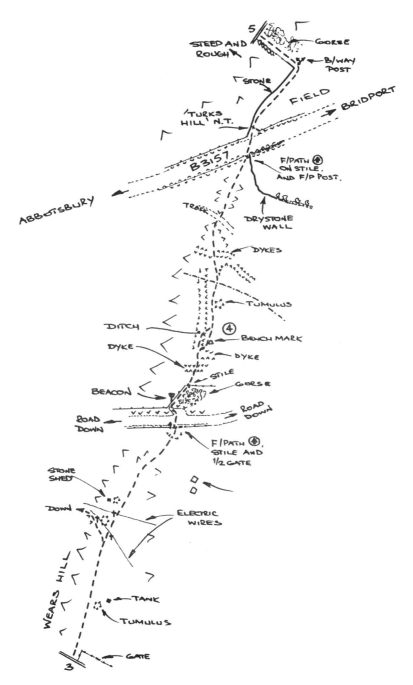

TURKS HILL TO COASTGUARD LOOKOUT

Carefully maintaining your balance - I hope - keep on down the gorse-clad path with the wire fence and bushes on your left.   After a while, you'll reach a turning off to your right which is signposted for "West Bexington" but keep on down, skirting around an intruding clump of hawthorns which causes you to lose the fence for a few yards.   Rejoining the fence, go over the stile into a downhill field and keep on down into the bottom LH corner of the hedged field with a pine-shielded bungalow in the enclosure on your right.

Go over the stile with the painted yellow arrow, next to a field gate, and aim down towards the farmhouse.   This direction will lead you to an exit farm gate, with another painted arrow, in the bottom corner of this field, after a cattle trough and next to a gate into the adjacent field.   A ditch comes down the field next to the hedge and runs under the track on the other side of the gate.   Join the track, past another trough, and follow it past a pit and the farm outbuildings and barns of East Bexington Farm.   As the firm track bends right past the barns, another Footpath signpost next to the fence up on your left points back to "Hill Fort" and on to "Chesil Beach". Cross the main farm track which leads to the farmhouse on your right and go into a downhill track with grass up the middle, a wide verge and hedge on its left and a fenced paddock on the right.

Go through the gate at the bottom and bend right/left to follow the track down with a ditch and hedge on your right.   As the hedge gives way to another fence, the track bends back left/right, still with the ditch, and leads you down to a short stretch of fence-enclosed track, over a main drainage ditch and onto the old tarmac lane which serves the farmsteads between Abbotsbury and West Bexington.   A stone "Coast Path" sign confirms that it is 1.1/2 miles back up to the Hill Fort.

The sea is very close at hand now but a brief diversion onto the shingle will convince you that it's too difficult to walk very far on it.   So stay on the tarmac lane with the banked ditch on your left, passing several "No Parking" passing-places on your right.   There are many run-off ditches from the steep fields on your left joining the main ditch and running under the lane to beach outfalls.   Alongside the second field ditch, a gravel drive turns up to East Bexington Dairy House.

Follow the long lane and, just after a beach access barrier, you meet the first hedge of tamarisk - a salt water and wind-resistant, deciduous hedge with feathery branches and masses of pink flowers in the summer (Sorry, I mean "abundant racemes of small flowers" - Royal Horticultural Society's Encyclopedia).   There are plenty of these tamarisk bushes along this lane and all the way into Abbotsbury and St Catherine's Hill and they are quite a feature of the Strangways Estate.

On the left side of the lane, the Coastguard Lookout stands next to the row of Castle Hill Cottages, their gardens and their garages.

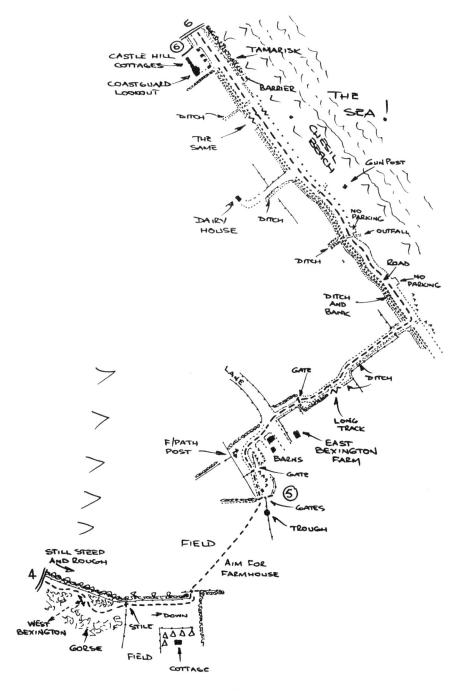

STAGE 6

COASTGUARD LOOKOUT TO ST CATHERINE'S HILL

The ditch which had accompanied the tamarisk hedge has now crossed to the field side and soon disappears completely, only to reappear after the road T-junction.   After the drive to the "Old Castle Laundry" and cottage, the next field is the last before the direct road to Abbotsbury via the famous Sub-Tropical Gardens.   To take that way will exclude you from a pleasant stroll past the Fleet Nature Reserve and across fields on your way to St Catherine's chapel but, if you're really weary, it gets you straight back to Abbotsbury in the company of dozens of visitors' cars.

The broken stone wall up on the hillside is all that remains of an earlier attempt by the Strangways to build a castellated house in addition to the manor house near the Abbey.   Sadly, the propensity for the soil to slide towards the sea, as demonstrated high in this field, caused the property to be abandoned - and demolished in 1934.

Now, call at the car park's conveniences for a wash and brush up before your return to Abbotsbury.   From the car park, go over the footbridge to the lane which runs parallel with the beach and follow the tamarisk hedge.   For the convenience of the less able, there is a wooden track from this bridge to the top of Chesil Beach but leave it for others because you have already enjoyed far superior views of the beach and, when you get up into the fields again, you will have superior views once more.

Follow the shingle-covered track alongside the tamarisk hedge until, just before a path bears off into the "Fleet Nature Reserve", you get a temporary view of St Catherine's chapel across the lynchets in the field over the hedge and fence on your left.   As your route approaches the chapel, the hills become too steep to see it and, when you emerge onto the hilltop, its great bulk comes as something of a surprise.

At the Coast Path stone, follow the direction towards "Swannery 1.1/4" along the track which bends left to a small Bridleway-arrowed gate leading onto an enclosed track.   A farm gate leads into the low field between your route and the reed beds. Follow the grassy, possibly rutted or muddy, track along the hedge until you reach a gate on your left and a large ditch/stream which runs under the turning to the RH gate.

The track which goes straight on leads to Abbotsbury but it misses the chapel and I don't recommend it now that you've come this far.   However, you can use it for a complete circuit of St Catherine's Hill on another occasion so I've walked it myself and included instructions on this Stage map .   These are - Keep going, with gates into the LH fenced field and along a banked, fenced field on your right, until you come to a Footpath and Bridleway-signed RH turning to a gate which crosses your path. Go through the gate and up the hedge and tree-lined track onto Stage 7.

Having dismissed that option, go over the RH stile next to the gate into its adjacent field .   Follow the edge of this level field, over a hump in the middle, past a cattle trough in the RH fence and past a wooden seat and a horse-jump, to the bottom RH corner.   Over the stile near the dry-stone wall and next to the gate in the corner, go through the opening in the wall and over the next stile which leads into another long field.   Follow the level path, past another seat near the far right corner, with the reed beds spread out over the wet field on your right and with white poplars shimmering in the woods ahead.   Turn left at the end of this field and follow the stone wall up, past a gate, to a stile which leads into another field with a banked hedge on your right.

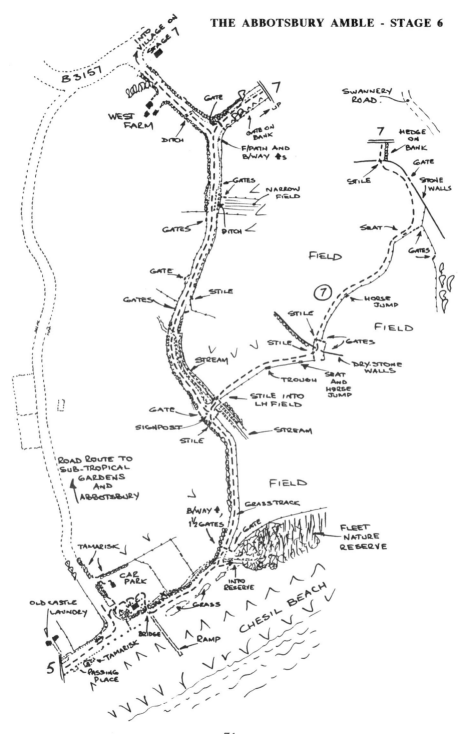

INTO VILLAGE ON STAGE 7

B3157

WEST FARM

DITCH

GATE

GATE ON BANK

7

UP

F/PATH AND B/WAY ↓s

SWANNERY ROAD.

7

HEDGE ON BANK

GATE

STILE

STONE WALLS

GATES

NARROW FIELD

GATES

DITCH

GATE

GATES

STILE

STREAM

SEAT

GATES

FIELD

7

HORSE JUMP

STILE

STILE

GATES

FIELD

STILE

TROUGH

DRY STONE WALLS

SEAT AND HORSE JUMP

STILE INTO LH FIELD

GATE

SIGNPOST

STILE

STREAM

ROAD ROUTE TO SUB-TROPICAL GARDENS AND ABBOTSBURY

FIELD

GRASS TRACK

B/WAY ↓ 1½ GATES

GATE

FLEET NATURE RESERVE

TAMARISK

CAR PARK

INTO RESERVE

OLD CASTLE LAUNDRY

GRASS

CHESIL BEACH

BRIDGE

RAMP

5

TAMARISK

PASSING PLACE

71

STAGE 7

ST CATHERINE'S HILL TO ABBOTSBURY

First of all, let's finish the track which missed the chapel completely but which goes around its North edge - Follow the banked and hedged track, past a high RH gate and past "Smugglers" on the left, to a T-junction. Turn left at the Footpath-signed corner and follow the track straight into West Street where you turn right for the start point of the "Ilchester Arms". Actually, you could use Stage 6 and 7 maps to make a shorter circular walk around St Catherine's hill and include a visit to the chapel.

Everybody else - You should be standing in a low field, next to a banked hedge, waiting for instructions. The drive to The Swannery is beyond the hedge and the small wood on your right as you continue along the edge of the field. Bearing left to follow the hedge, and fence now, you soon reach an old, bare hedge bank which crosses your path and retains a single old hawthorn bush. There is a stile in the RH hedge whilst a Footpath arrow points to "Swannery". However, turn left beyond the bank and head up the field towards a Permissive Path-signed stile in the wire fence with a few hawthorns scattered therein. Over the stile, a stone sign confirms your direction - straight up the steep grassy banks and slipping topsoil of the hill, to another stile in the wire fence which comes up next to the crow-filled woods on your right and then runs round towards your left. The stile stands next to a horse-jump whilst another signpost points vaguely left of the correct route for the chapel.

Keep on up the steep slope and, nearing the top, you cross a narrow dyke and a green track which comes from your left. Slightly out of breath, you will be quite unprepared for the sudden appearance of St Catherine's chapel and, as you approach the stile towards its LH end, the sandstone structure with its 4 ft thick walls begins to loom massively ahead. It was built either during the time of Abbot Henry de Thorpe who died in 1376 or Abbot William Cerne who ruled the Abbey between 1376 and 1401. At the dissolution of 1536-39, it was not destroyed because of its conspicuous use to sailors as a landmark. The chapel is dedicated to St Catherine, a high-born, scholarly lady of Alexandria who, for her faith, was tortured on a wheel and then beheaded in 290 AD during the reign of Emperor Maximinus. Her death is commemorated on 15th November.

Leave the chapel by the corner kissing gate and join the grass and red-soiled track to descend towards the dry-stone wall. With fine views to the village and Abbey ahead of you, follow the track past the kissing gates in the stone wall and round its bottom end where it bends left and continues to descend, passing two cattle troughs and a walled enclosure of stone barns and a long shed on your left. A deep, grassy gulley follows the stone wall away to your right behind you. Go through the kissing gate and join the track which comes, between the barn walls and a high banked field, from your left. Follow the track straight on with a stone wall on your right and the banked field on your left. Where a gate and stile lead up into the LH field, the bush-covered path on your right leads to the back of the "Ilchester Arms". Keep straight on, past a gated house drive and between stone walls, to emerge between the Post Office and the Pottery onto the pavement of "West Street". There is a small, iron-fenced garden with a couple of benches opposite your emergence so, if you have any sandwiches left, you could sit there and finish them off before your final end-of-day collapse. Really, you could sit quietly awhile before going for your bus or your other transport, remembering some of the wonderful sights you have seen today and determined to come back and explore further another time.

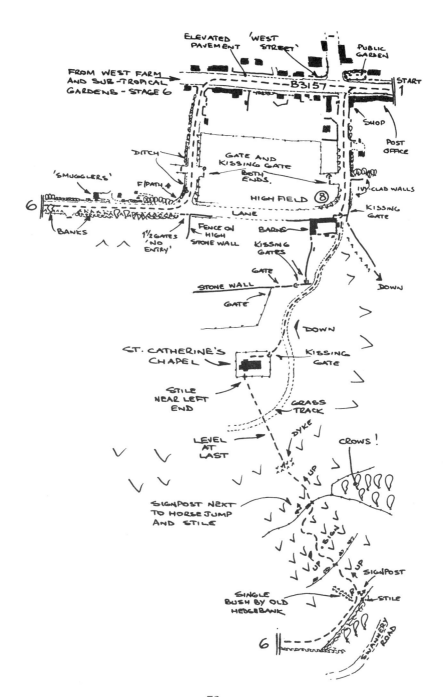

73

Top: St Catherine's Chapel, Abbotsbury .   Page 72

Bottom: Smedmore House, Kimmeridge.   Page 88

PART FIVE - THE ENCOMBE ENCOUNTER

INTRODUCTION

How could any book purport to introduce anybody to the delights of Dorset without including at least one walk in the Isle of Purbeck.   I know it can't be indisputable but I consider the view from Swyre Head (one of two Swyre Heads actually) to be a classic and one of the greatest sea, cliff, down and farm landscapes of this beautiful county.

Wilts and Dorset buses Nos. 143 and 144 from Poole and Swanage call frequently at the "Scott Arms" on the top of Kingston Hill, a short stroll from the start and finish of these walks at Plantation Car Park (Reference SY953795 on O S Map No. 195).

Hang gliders launch themselves from the slopes of Smedmore Hill to join the crows and kestrels who regularly patrol these hills in search of food.   They must all enjoy the superlative views along the Purbeck coast and savour the tranquillity as they pass over a pair of typical Purbeck stately homes - both of which you will see from similar vantage points.

The churches of Kingston and Kimmeridge are both worth a visit and are completely different - not only in the huge variation in their sizes.   Kimmeridge village benefits from a very popular tea shop/restaurant which is frequently packed in the summer and much patronised by climbers, hikers, geologists, sub-aqua divers and wind-surfers at all times of the year.

The longer route brings you close to the first on-shore oilfield to be developed on this coast - but don't worry.   All that is visible is a nodding donkey and a couple of small collection tanks inside a wire-fenced enclosure.   This isn't the only industrial venture based at Kimmeridge.   The shale has been known to contain oil for centuries, (With the cliffs sometimes spontaneously igniting, it would be difficult not to notice) and earlier exploitation caused the bankruptcy of one Sir William Clavell, whose tower is so prominent on the cliff edge.   Actually, his alum production and glass-making weren't all that successful, either.

For your complete enjoyment, I have introduced alternative Routes which will enable you to plan long or short walks or to change your mind on the way round.

THE ALTERNATIVES

By starting outside the "Scott Arms" (Reference SY956796 on O S Map No. 195), near to the bus stops, all of the Routes share the first few Stages but diverge at Swyre Head or Kimmeridge for long or short variations as listed.   Just two Wilts and Dorset buses serve Kingston but they are quite frequent - Nos. 143 and 144 from Poole, Wareham and Swanage which run Mondays to Saturdays, except Bank Holidays.

ROUTE 1: Total distance 9.1/4 miles.   This is the "Total" Route which starts with the high lane from Kingston to the gates of the Encombe Estate, follows tracks and high grassland to the most magnificent view from Swyre Head barrow and then swings West to follow the top of Smedmore Hill all the way into Kimmeridge.   This charming little village, with its church, Post Office and Tea Rooms leads to the cross-fields path to Kimmeridge Bay whence your Route turns up to the cliff top "Dorset Coast Path" route for two miles to Houns Tout.   To be perfectly fair, Houns Tout rises 400 ft from your starting point at the outlet from Encombe Valley and it isn't gradual, if you know what I mean.   It's a killer (Well, it makes the heart pound a bit and the legs begin to give out) - so you've been warned.   The final leg of Route 1 is along the wide, gentle greensward above Encombe House and through the woods to Kingston.   A wonderful day's walking with loads of interest and wonderful views along the way..

ROUTE 2: Total distance 5.1/2 miles.   At Swyre Head, this Route turns down the steep slope of Smedmore Hill and crosses farmland of Swalland Farm straight to the cliff top route of the Coast Path.   Thence it rejoins Route 1 for the climb up Houns Tout and back to Kingston.   It therefore shares the steep return of Houns Tout which I would only recommend for fitter walkers.

ROUTE 3: Total distance 6.3/4 miles.   To avoid the Houns Tout struggle, Route 3 brings you back up Smedmore Hill to Swyre Head but, although it isn't as steep or as high as Houns Tout, it also requires some degree of fitness.   Leaving Route 1 at Kimmeridge to avoid the Coast Path route, this alternative follows the valley lane between the ridge and the sea visiting Smedmore House and Swalland Farm on the way back to climb Smedmore Hill back to Swyre Head and the top road back to Kingston. Apart from the climb up Smedmore Hill - a 350 ft climb but only the last 150 ft being very, very steep - this is quite an easy Route which offers wonderful views on the way.

STAGE MILEAGES

STAGE	MILES	TOTAL MILES
ROUTE 1:		
1 Kingston to Encombe Gate	1	1
2 Encombe Gate to Swyre Head	1	2
3 Swyre Head to Kimmeridge Hill	1.25	3.25
4 Kimmeridge Hill to Cliff Top Car Park	1	4.25
5 Cliff Top Car Park to Clavell's Hard	1.75	6
6 Clavell's Hard to Rope Head Lake	.75	6.75
7 Rope Head Lake to Houns Tout	1	7.75
8 Houns Tout to Encombe Wood	1	8.75
1 Encombe Wood to Kingston	.50	9.25

STAGE MILEAGES - CONTINUED

ROUTE 2:

1 - 2 as Route 1 to Swyre Head	2	2
2a Swyre Head to Swalland Field	.50	2.50
6 Swalland Field to Rope Head Lake	.50	3
7, 8 and 1 - as Route 1 to Kingston	2.50	5.50

ROUTE 3:

1 - 3 as Route 1 to Kimmeridge Hill	3.25	3.25
4 Kimmeridge Hill to Smedmore Gates	.25	3.50
4a Smedmore Gates to Smedmore House	.50	3.75
2a Smedmore House to Swyre Head	1	4.75
2 - 1 as Route 1 to/from Kingston	2	6.75

ROUTE LAYOUT:

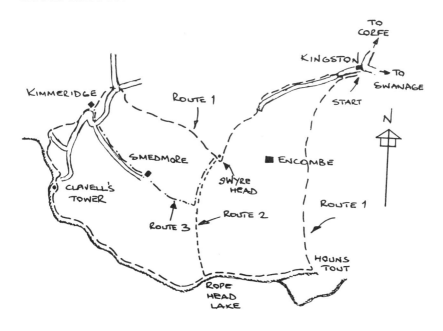

STAGE 1

KINGSTON TO ENCOMBE GATE

Listed in the Domesday Book as *Chingestone* (the king's village), Kingston was leased to Shaftesbury Abbey and 200 years later it was known as Kyngeston Abbatisse. Kingston stands on the edge of the folded chalk Purbeck bed, looking down on the ruins of Corfe Castle and the lovely stone village which grew up around the castle, parts of which date back to pre-William the Conqueror.

Start outside (yes, outside) the "Scott Arms", facing the long, stone old farrier's shed on the other side of West Street. Turn right up the hill to the Post Office which stands on the elevated stone pavement opposite South Street. St James' Church stands high in the churchyard on the far LH corner at a height of nearly 450 ft - no wonder it's so prominent on the skyline. Its size appears over-generous for the population of Kingston when it was finished in 1880 after 7 years' work for stonemasons and the local quarry. It is one of the last churches designed by G E Street and it is built of the local Purbeck and Portland stone with a vaulted chancel and a lofty central tower. The fittings are also by Street and the wrought ironwork is very fine. It appears that the quarry's customers went elsewhere during the building of the church, never to return, and quarrying in Kingston came to an abrupt end when the church was finished.

Ignore the Footpath which turns right after the Post Office and carry on up West Street, with St James' on your left, past the last cottages and a forest track on your right, into the forested lane where your speed is now unrestricted. Kingston House drive turns sharply down to your left whilst the left fork is the return route from the Coast Path and Houns Tout for both Routes 1 and 3. The text covering this return is in Stage 8 but it'll be quite clear when you're ready for it. Now, keeping straight on, (signed for Encombe House), you instantly pass "The Plantation" car park with mixed beech and pine woods on either side. After opposite, overgrown, "Private" tracks into the woods, you leave the stone wall-enclosed woods and the road continues, slightly up and down, across a vast sloping field for about 1/2 mile with fine views right to Corfe Castle and the twin ridges, one each side of the castle.

After a couple of passing places and a few lonely hawthorns, you will see the 40 ft obelisk which was erected in 1835 "in honour of Sir William Scott, created Baron Stowell". The first stone was laid by Lady F I Bankes, younger daughter of John Scott, the 1st Earl of Eldon who bought Encombe House in 1807. Now you know where the "Scott Arms" connection fits into the Encombe Estate.

There are tempting views ahead to the barrow on Swyre Head, just past the LH end of the woods which run along the top of Encombe Valley. The beech wood over on your left is growing on the nearer slopes of the same valley. After the slight left bend in the road, the road descends between a low LH field edged with a row of beech bushes and trees and a RH fenced and stone walled field. Keep on down to the end of this field and, level with the gate into the next RH field there is a car parking area on your left. A stone plaque in the corner gives some detail about the Coast Path. The road continues towards "Orchard Hill Farm" but you want to turn down, between the stone pillared gateposts, signed for "Encombe House and Lower Encombe". Through the gate, keep straight on - not down the long "Private. No Footpath" drive but across to the sheep pens, the farm gate and the smaller gate with the "Dogs on Lead" sign . This gate leads onto an uphill, stony farm track in a wide, grassy sheep-grazing field.

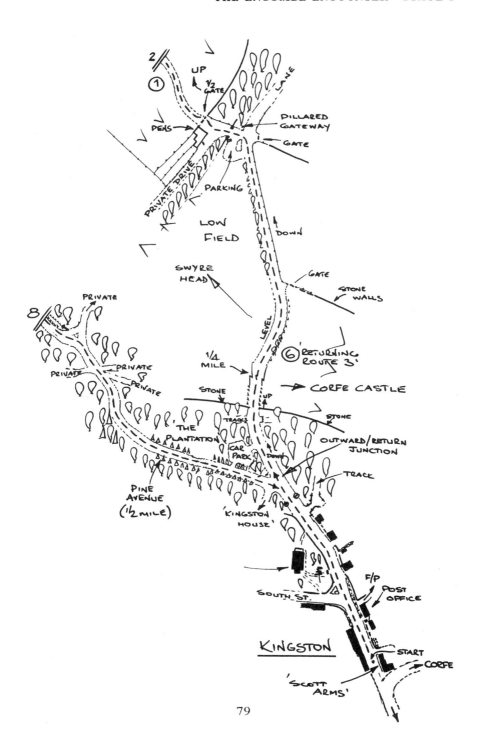

79

STAGE 2

ENCOMBE GATE TO SWYRE HEAD

Keep on up the stony track with grass up the middle until the stone-walled wood over on your right, known as 'The Belt', comes across to meet you.   On the way up, you pass a couple of grass tracks going up to your left and the wire fence comes across to meet your track in the top corner of the field.   At a junction of gates and wooden fences, go through the Bridleway-arrowed half-gate and sit for a while on the stone seat on the other side.   Another track turns down to a gated field and then continues down a grassy gulley into Encombe Valley.   Stay up on the high greensward and follow the dry-stone wall along the valley top with the mixed 'Polar Wood' behind it. This wood is filled with bluebells in late spring and they are at just the right eye level to look like a blue mist.   By the way, the wire fences which seem to duplicate the boundaries provided by the stone walls are there to stop the sheep from breaking down the loose stones.   The wall builder on the Strangways Estate at Abbotsbury (Walk 4) told me that sheep are particularly adept at destroying dry-stone walls.

Anyway, with Encombe House, its stable block and its walled gardens appearing at the foot of the gorse-covered slopes on your left, perhaps a little detail wouldn't go amiss.   The property was sold to George Pitt of Stratfieldsaye (The 1st Duke of Wellington's home from 1817) in 1734 but he died the same year and the house passed to his son, John Pitt - an amateur architect.   Using ideas gleaned from the Palladian style and from the works of Vanbrugh and Hawksmoor, John redesigned the house and it was rebuilt by 1770, retaining some of the original property.   John's son, William Moreton Pitt sold the house to John Scott, later 1st Earl of Eldon, in 1807 and, since 1870, under John, 3rd Earl of Eldon, extensive internal alterations were made.   The stables are early 19thC and were built by the 2nd Earl of Eldon.

Now, enjoying your stroll along the top of the valley, the greensward soon includes a track but just keep going, very slightly uphill now.   After a stone step into the woods, the track bears left round the head of the valley towards the back of 'Swyre Wood'.   As the track disappears, keep swinging round to the left and you will find a stone against the fence between you and the Swyre Head bowl barrow.   The Royal Commission on Historical Monuments advises us that this barrow stands more than 600 ft above sea level, that it is 83 ft diameter and 8 ft high whilst the stone tells us that it is 2 miles back to Kingston and 1.3/4 miles to Kimmeridge.   Approaching the stile in the corner, be prepared for a most breath-taking coastline view.   I've seen it several times but it never fails to send a tingle down my spine.   A stone seat just past the barrow gives you a fine opportunity to savour the view and, when you have imbibed fully, you have to decide whether to continue to Kimmeridge or take the shorter Route 2 straight down to the Coast Path and return via Houns Tout.

Everybody return over the stile and I'll assume that you are going straight on - *so* **Route 2** *walkers scan down to your instructions in italics.*   Follow the fence and then the stone wall across the level field.   Go through the 1/2 gate with the Bridleway arrow into the next field, keep following the wall down and go through another half-gate next to a farm gate which leads onto a fence-enclosed, rutted grass track.

ROUTE 2: *Turn left and go over the Permissive Path-signed stile onto the Footpath-signed slopes of Smedmore Hill.   Carefully descend the gorse-clad path into a wide, bumpy field of coarse grass and sheep until your route is edged by wire-fenced fields.*

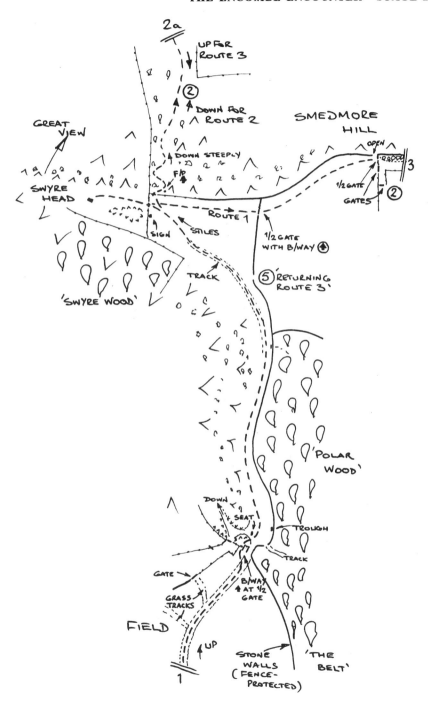

SWYRE HEAD TO SWALLAND FIELD and SMEDMORE HOUSE TO SWYRE HEAD

ROUTE 2: (Still in italics)   Keep on down the fenced-in field to the narrowing bottom end and go through the gateway or over the stile on its left.   Cross the group of tractor tracks with a farm track on your right and go down into a rutted, grassy, fence-enclosed track past another stile and gateway.   Keep going down the track to a third stile/gateway arrangement and into a T-junction of tractor tracks with the main track to Swalland Farm down on your right.   There is another stile to the right of a very large gate facing you.   This has a stone sign for "Coast Path and Rope Head Lake".   Go over the stile and follow the RH banked hedge and fence down the field. Now turn to Stage 6 to continue.

ROUTE 3: Keep straight on, with the walls of the kitchen garden on your left and the white-railed gateway into "Smedmore House Camping and Caravan Site" down on your right.   A "Private" drive turns away to your left after the garden walls and you now continue up the lane with a hedge, then a small wood, on your left and with a ditch and mixed trees on your right.   After the LH wood, a gate into the field opens onto a Footpath signed "To The Top of The Hill" - the destination couldn't be clearer. You can get back up to the top of Smedmore Hill that way if you want, but I'm going straight on to Swalland Farm.

Slightly uphill, with overgrown fences to right and left, the RH verge widens at the top of the slope and there is a gate into the RH field.   Descending now, the lane bears left as you reach gated fields either side, just before "Chaldecotts" - the house on your left.   Keep going, uphill slightly again, over a ditch which runs from and into overgrown, scrubby patches and climb up towards Swalland Farm with a hedge on your left and a fence on your right.

Walk carefully through the barns and cow-sheds of Swalland Farm, now on concrete, and past the farmhouse and its low-walled garden on your right.   The concrete now gives way to a rising, stony, chalky track between a LH wire fence and a RH hedge with a track turning into the RH field.   Keep on up the steeper track until a stile turns off to your right, signed for "Coast Path and Rope Head Lake".

Walk into the junction of tractor tracks and turn left, past a stile and an open gateway, into a fence-enclosed, rutted track.   At the end, go past another stile/gateway into a tractor-rutted area with another farm track going to your left.   Keep straight on up, past a third stile/gateway into a widening, marshy and bumpy field of rough grass. As the LH fence ends, keep going up the steep side of Smedmore Hill and follow the thin, bending path through the gorse bushes to the top fence where you will find a Footpath-arrowed post and a stile in the top corner.   Go over the stile and you're back on Swyre Head.   Have another sit on the stone bench you found earlier - you've earned it.

When you've rested, just go back to Kingston the way you came this morning - using Maps 2 and 1 if you can't remember the way.

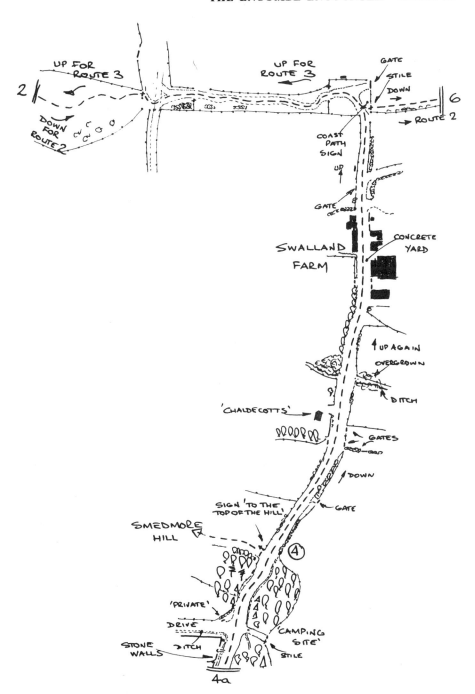

STAGE 3

SWYRE HEAD TO KIMMERIDGE HILL

Keep following the enclosed track, now with hawthorns on your left and generally with the same superb view towards Tyneham Cap and Gad Cliff. These limestone cliffs stand above the village of Tyneham which was evacuated by the Army during the 2nd World War so that they could use the area for tank and weapons training. They're still there and the small, stone village is in ruins although attempts are being made to retain and repair the buildings and the church which are still standing. It's a lovely spot and much visited by holidaymakers. Actually, when most people have gone home, it's also much visited by foxes, deer and buzzards.

But I digress. After a while, there are some steps over the stone wall which lead onto a signed Footpath to Smedmore. Where the path emerges onto the Smedmore road below, there is a sign which unequivocally says "To The Top of The Hill".

Keep going and, after a bend to the left, a gate in a stone wall crosses your path, after which another gate opens onto the slopes on your left. You are now out of the enclosed track and in a stony field which drops down to the right and also straight ahead to another gate in a facing stone wall. Go through this gate into a steeply rising field and follow the wall up to the top. After a level stretch, with views ahead and slightly right to Steeple Church in the valley and Creech Arch on the top of the ridge beyond, the field begins to descend. From here on, it's all downhill into Kimmeridge village. Go through the gate onto another fence and wall-enclosed, rutted, stony track which descends ever steeper around a right and left bend. On the way, you pass a scrub and gorse-packed area on your left but keep clear. Somewhere in there is the top edge of a quarry which opens out onto the road down into Kimmeridge. Follow the track around the LH banked and RH fenced bend to the bottom and go through the final gate.

At a junction of tracks, go straight down into a tarmac lane and turn left, between banked bushes on your left and the ditch and hedge on your right. Follow the lane down to a T-junction with a "Farmhouse B & B" sign on the RH corner. The left turn goes to the quarry and Kimmeridge by road but cross straight over to the stile which is signposted "Kimmeridge 1/4". The half-gate just up the hill leads onto the Footpath to Tyneham Cap and village.

Go over the Kimmeridge stile and head down the bush and gorse-bordered grassy gulley which brings you out onto the steep slopes of another sheep field. Aim for the gate in the iron fence, just to the LH end of the church below. St Nicholas' church is very small, very old and built of rubble stone with ashlar edges to doors and windows. The nave is 12thC and the 13thC South porch is original. The bellcote and buttresses were added to the West end in the 15thC whilst the church was extensively rebuilt in 1872.

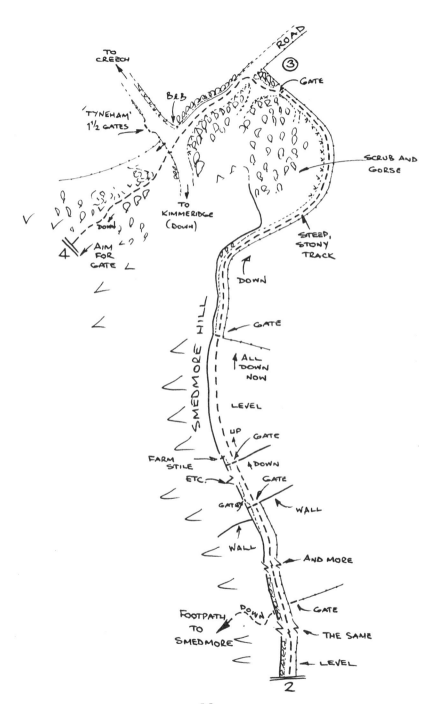

STAGE 4

KIMMERIDGE HILL TO CLIFF TOP CAR PARK or SMEDMORE GATES

Go through the iron kissing gate after the ditch footbridge and walk down the (sometimes slippery) stone flagged path of St Nicholas' churchyard with the fence and stone wall of "The Old Parsonage" on your left.   This fine stone house was built in 1837 in the 17thC Jacobean style.   Down the steps, a wide track goes right into Kimmeridge Farm and there is a seat tucked into the stone wall on your left from where you can get your bearings.   The front entrance of Kimmeridge Farm house carries the shield-of-arms of Mansel - predecessors of the owners of Smedmore House.

ROUTE 3: If you want to go back to Kingston without using the Coast Path or the steep climb up Houns Tout, keep going left along the rising road, past The Old Parsonage gates, and keep straight on when the road does a hairpin left.   Follow the hedged and fenced lane to the white gates which are signed "Private Road. Smedmore and Swalland" and turn to Stage 4a which is just for you.

ROUTE 1: But, if you're going all the way on Route 1, follow the road down into Kimmeridge with the walled playing field on your right and the Seven Taps Restaurant, Tea Rooms and Post Office on your left.   (I can recommend the cream teas - whatever the time).   The next gateway on the left leads into the Village Hall, from where a Footpath runs across fields to join the Smedmore track on Route 3. However, keep on down between stone, thatched cottages on your immediate right and houses behind hedges on your left.   When there are no more cottages on your right, go over the Footpath-signed stile into a field which runs down by the garden fence of the last cottage.   (Alternatively, you could always run the gauntlet of cars and stay on the top road to the Car Park).   Follow the garden fence down to a footbridge across a stream with a stile at either end.   Over the shady bridge, another stile leads into trees on your right but turn left here and follow the winding ditch, past a wood and a streamside row of willows, to a pair of Footpath-arrowed stiles close to a low, ruined stone barn in the brambles and bushes on your right.

Over the stiles, keep following the ditch, with a fenced field beyond it, to another stile and a farm gate.   This time, there is a small, fenced enclosure of dense bushes with a less ruinous barn perched on the far edge.   Over the double Footpath-arrowed stile, go past the barn and follow the tree-bedecked, winding ditch past one final LH gate.   Zig-zag right/left up, past a sunken ditch which comes from across the field on your right, to go through a Footpath-arrowed farm gate and join the lane to the Oil Extraction enclosure.   On the hawthorn-edged lane, turn left at the signpost "Beach and Coast Path" and go through a gate which crosses the lane just before handy conveniences on your right.   A stile in the LH fence only leads up to the Toll Road.

Up the lane, follow the RH bushes round into the car park and stroll around the seaward end, past or stopping at any loitering Ice Cream vans.   At the far end of the car park, go through a narrow, 50 yards long, gap between the bushes shielding the house up on your left and the edge (bushed or clear) of the cliffs on your right. Emerging into the divers' and sail-boarders' car park, there is a path down to the quay and the beach immediately on your right but, for the Coast Path, you have to go straight on through the parking area.

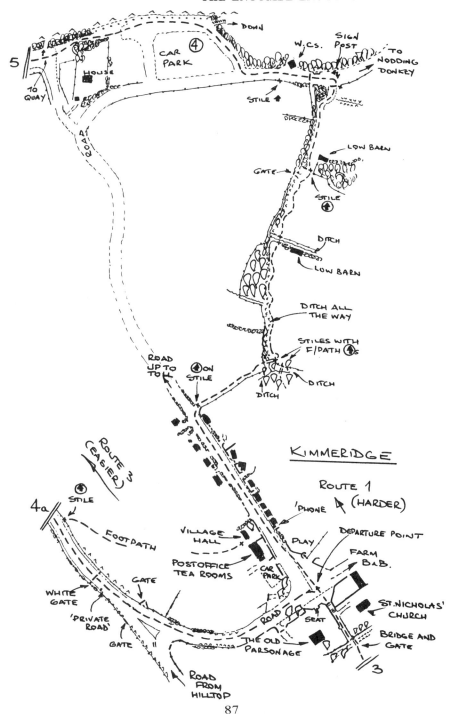

SMEDMORE GATES TO SMEDMORE HOUSE

There are fine views of Kimmeridge village and the sea from this part of the lane and, as you're on your way back, you may fancy a cream tea. I can recommend the Seven Taps Restaurant, Tea Rooms and Post Office in the village so, if you go over the stile which you have just passed and head back across the fields, you will come out at the Village Hall, next door to the Post Office.

However, there will come a time when I won't be able to get a cream tea there myself because there won't be any room, so forget it and keep on going, with the lane descending a little around a slight left hand bend and with fenced fields on either side. After gates on your right and a gateway on your left, a stream comes out of the narrow wood on your left and runs into the LH ditch. Another gate opens into each of the LH and RH fields before the lane passes a couple of hawthorns in the wider RH verge. As a ditch crosses under the road, the RH, wide grass track leads down to "Barn Dairy" farmhouse and barns.

Now, keep on going with a ditch, fence and hedge on your left and a verge, fence and hedge on your right. When another ditch runs under the lane from the edge of some trees on your left into a tree-lined ditch on your right, you go between two large Scots pines into the drive proper of Smedmore House. The tarmac drive ascends between grass verges and wire fences with stiles into private fields, passing a bulky, round yew tree on the way. Reaching the top of the slope, Smedmore House looks superb, grand but not over-grand. It was built in the 17thC by Sir William Clavell of stone with a stone slate roof. Entirely remodelled in the early 18thC, the "new and sophisticated South West elevation" was added. This includes the lovely rounded bow window elevations which are facing you. A new range of reception and entrance rooms were built across the North West end in 1761 and a kitchen wing was added. On rare occasions, Smedmore House opens its gardens to the public under the National Gardens scheme. If you get the chance to visit, do so. It'll be a splendid afternoon and you'll love the intimate gardens.

Now, follow the lane around to the right, away from the house with some fine pine trees in the lawn near you. A track turns off right, alongside a mixed deciduous and pine wood, down to a gated field entrance. Keep straight on with a ditch and the stone garden wall of Smedmore House on your left. The low wall grants lovely views of the tree and shrub-planted garden on the South side of the house.

Now turn to Stage 2a to continue along the lane for Route 3's return to Swyre Head

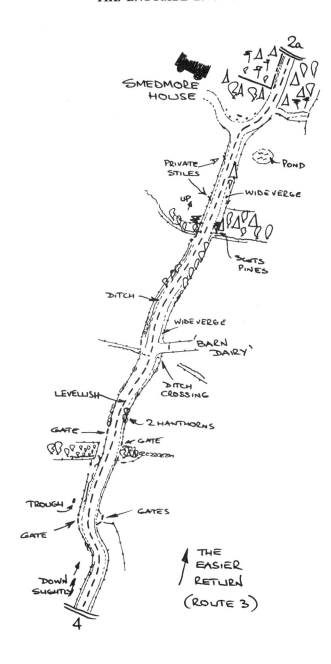

STAGE 5

CLIFF TOP CAR PARK TO CLAVELL'S HARD

Leaving the car park past another toilet block, turn down the tarmac track which comes down from your left. The signpost in front of the banked trees points the way for the Coast Path. Over the stream, walk down the hill and past the right turn into the bottom Emergency services' and divers' car park. After the concrete tank defences, turn up the steep steps which are cut into the LH hillside by another Coast Path sign. At first, the steps are within dense bushes but you soon emerge into the light at a fenced LH field and with the close cliff edge on your right.

This is a bit of a struggle after all the gentle, level and downhill, strolling you've enjoyed so far, so take it slowly. After a few more scattered steps and uphill climbing on grass, the field fence turns left and you're almost within gasping distance of Clavell's Tower. Have a good look around the tower and enjoy the views across Kimmeridge Bay, busy with windsurfers, rock pool explorers, divers and geologists - it'll give you an excuse to get your breath back - but keep away from the cliff edge.

This is the first warning about the cliff edge but when you realise that the fence replaces earlier fences which have disappeared to accommodate the ever-retreating Coast Path, you'll have some idea of how unstable are these cliffs of Kimmeridge clay. The circular tower, a folly, was built by the Rev John Richards, who assumed the name of Clavell on inheriting Smedmore in 1817 and died in 1833. It is built of brick and rubble-stone and rendered.

Now, continue past the Coast Path sign-stone which tells you that this cliff top path leads to "Chapmans Pool 3.3/4". You turn off back to Kingston before Chapmans Pool - but only just before - so you're in for a most enjoyable coastal walk with beautiful sea views and interesting rock strata in the cliffs from time to time, with the mingled calls of gulls on the seaward side and skylarks over the fields.

I'll keep written instructions to a bare minimum along this section of the walk because of the proximity of the high cliff edge but suffice it to say that the path follows the contours of the land, crosses emerging streams as they plummet over the edge, and sometimes hugs the fence where more recent landslips have brought the cliff edge too close to the path. To follow the text, stop to read it occasionally. Let caution be your watchword - but enjoy it!

When you arrive at a short section of narrow-gauge rail track hanging over the cliff edge, you have arrived at Clavell's Hard. This track is a remnant of a 19thC construction used for transporting bituminous shale which Clavell mined here.

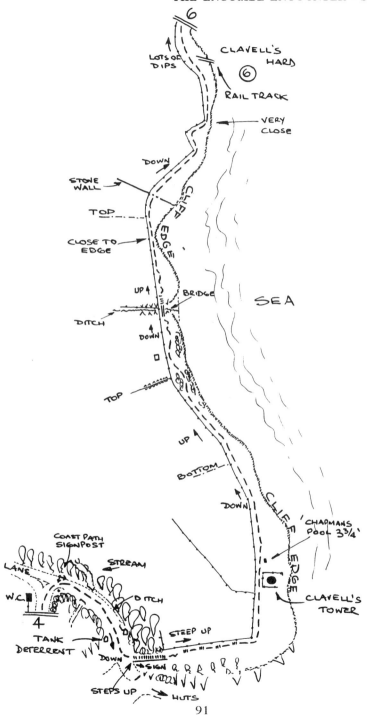

6

LOTS OF
DIPS

CLAVELL'S
HARD

6

RAIL TRACK

VERY
CLOSE

DOWN

STONE
WALL

TOP

CLIFF EDGE

CLOSE TO
EDGE

UP

BRIDGE

SEA

DITCH

DOWN

TOP

UP

BOTTOM

DOWN

CLIFF EDGE

CHAPMANS
POOL 3¾'

COAST PATH
SIGNPOST

LANE

STREAM

W.C.

DITCH

4

CLAVELL'S
TOWER

TANK
DETERRENT

STEEP UP

DOWN

SIGN

STEPS UP

HUTS

91

CLAVELL'S HARD (and SWALLAND FIELD) TO ROPE HEAD LAKE

This first part is only for those on *Route* 2 who came straight down from Swyre Head on Stage 2a without going to Kimmeridge:

ROUTE 2: Keep following the banked RH hedge and fence down to a dip in the field and then continue up and over a rise until you pass scrub and an overgrown hedge near the bottom end to reach a stile in the cliff top fence. Go over the stile and turn left to join Route 1 walkers at * below in the last paragraph. I've already warned the others not to go too near the edge of the cliffs because they're not very stable - as shown by the ever retreating fence and the brief explanation given two paragraphs down on this page. Near the cliff edges, don't walk along whilst reading!

ROUTE 1: After the rail track, a short descent brings you to one of the ditches as it runs out from the field and plunges over the cliff edge. This one has a footbridge with a handrail on the cliff side. After the bridge, go up and over a hump and you'll see another footbridge down the dip ahead of you. There is a deep, grassy slump here where you can stop for a while for a read - it seems quite stable at the moment.

If you look at the bed of the stream between the bridge and the cliff top, you'll see that it is running on top of the smooth limestone layer. This shows why the cliffs are so unstable. They consist of smooth, flat layers of this limestone between layers of bituminous shale and Kimmeridge clay. The first contains oil and the second is excessively slippery when wet. Water percolates through the shale and soaks into the clay but stops when it gets to the stone bed, lubricating the joint between the stone and the overlying clay/shale. Its own weight is enough to propel it downwards and outwards whenever the adhesion gives way.

"In the 17thC, Sir William Clavell proposed to extract alum from the layers of bituminous shale and also to use it, as the Romans had done before, as fuel for boiling sea water to extract salt. These enterprises, and plans to manufacture glass, using the shale for fuel, came to nothing. In the 19thC oil was, for a time, extracted from the shale, and an Act of 1847 gave powers to construct railways....inclined planes, causeways etc": D Maxwell's Unknown Dorset 1927.

Now, carry on up and over a long hill with some sections quite close to the edge. On the way down you will meet with the Route 2 walkers who come down the field to the stile next to the direction stone which says "Kimmeridge Bay 1.1/2 and Chapmans Pool 2.1/4". This is called Rope Head Lake but I don't know why - although there *is* a pond in the field between here and Swyre Head.

* Right, **ROUTES 1 AND 2** all together again. Go down the hill to a rough section where a ditch runs under the footbridge and out to the cliff edge. On the other side, the cliff top is a bit wider at first and, after a bend in the fence where the edge comes closer, the climb becomes steeper.

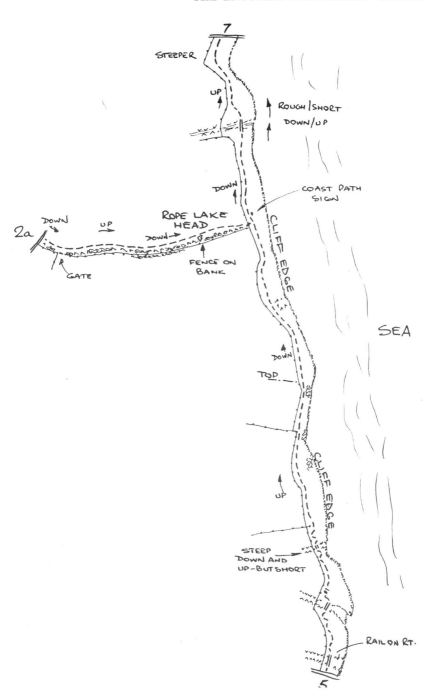

ROPE HEAD LAKE TO HOUNS TOUT

Descending again, cross a dry run-off and then a remnant of stone wall.   If you look forward and slightly left, you will see Eldon's Seat on the top of the hill.   When the land levels out, there are two more gulleys about 50 yards apart in rough grass and, when the fence bends left, you drop down into a wide, rough grassy area with a field facing you on the opposite slope.   Wend your way through the grass, veering towards the cliff, and climb up between the field and the cliff on a wide, grassy slope.

The slope becomes steeper until, at the top, Eldon's Seat is just along the edge of the fenced field away on your left.   The seat is made from a single block of limestone 8 ft by 4 ft with a second slab set up on edge to form a backrest, all on a stone podium.   It was laid by Lady E Repton, elder daughter of the 1st Earl of Eldon, on 15th October 1835.   Beside it is a memorial stone to Lord Chancellor Eldon's dog, Pincher, dated 1840.

Now, enjoy the next 1/4 mile descent because you're coming to the struggle up Houns Tout.   Descending steeply at first on grass, then up out of a small dip, the path levels out before descending once more, ever more steeply, until you reach the bottom where Encombe Valley arrives at the sea from its uppermost reaches around Encombe House. The valley is wooded and a stream which runs from the lakes is entrained within a stone culvert underneath the old drive, running out over the stone bed to drop down a waterfall onto the beach.   It is strange to see a pair of stone gate pillars with rusted iron fencing right on the edge of a drop over the cliff edge but this was once another entrance to Encombe Valley from a carriage drive which came round the cliffs from Chapmans Pool around this headland.   When you look at the massive slumping and landslips beyond the waterfall, you will get some idea of just how much land has disappeared over the years.

May I suggest that you sit and ponder for a few minutes - getting ready for the steep and tiring climb up Houns Tout.

Turning away from the cliff, follow the path in your original direction along the coast, through the trees and bushes and up a zig-zagging line until you come out onto open ground again with another field on your left.   The trees on your left continue all the way along the side of the valley to where you entered the estate through the Encombe Gates earlier today.

Use the slumped ground as steps and keep climbing the bush-covered slopes.   There is a little respite as the path drops briefly into a rough grassy, dippy area with much slumping of the whole cliff between you and the sea.

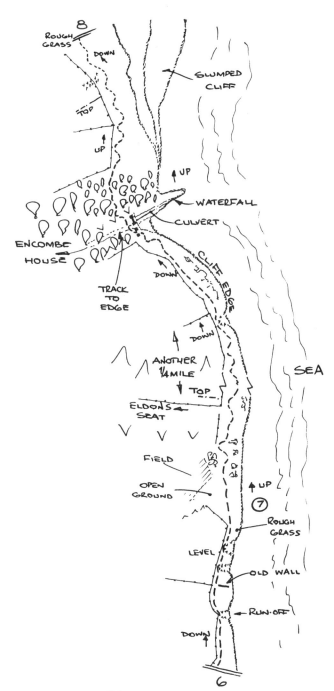

8

ROUGH GRASS

DOWN

SLUMPED CLIFF

TOP

UP

UP

WATERFALL

CULVERT

ENCOMBE HOUSE

DOWN

CLIFF EDGE

TRACK TO EDGE

DOWN

ANOTHER ¼ MILE

SEA

TOP

ELDON'S SEAT

FIELD

OPEN GROUND

UP

⑦

ROUGH GRASS

LEVEL

OLD WALL

RUN-OFF

DOWN

6

STAGE 8

HOUNS TOUT TO ENCOMBE WOOD

Now you begin the ultimate climb of the day.   The area is wide and grassy with some slumped 'steps' but there is little else I can say other than, "Look at the outcrop of weathered limestone on the top edge of Houns Tout overlooking the sea.   As it gets nearer, you'll know you're getting nearer the top".

Passing a section of old iron railing, you join another wire fence as you zig-zag up the hill - the Stage map shortens this bit just to make you feel that it's shorter than it really is.   However, when you get to the top, there is a wonderful, level and grassy stroll back to Kingston and, by the time that you reach the other end, you'll have fully recovered from this climb.

At the top, there is a stone seat for which thanks are due to Mr Byrne.   Resting here, you can see the Norman chapel on the cliff top at St Aldhelm's Head and, when you get up again, you will find the Coast Path stone indicates "1.3/4 miles to Kingston", "3 miles back to Kimmeridge" and "2.1/4 miles to Swyre Head" (via Rope Head Lake). Turn back to the stile in the corner between the fence and the dry-stone wall and climb over onto the wide greensward at the top of Encombe Valley.   The most level part is about 20 yards from the wall as you follow the edge of the ridge back home and there are several stone blocks near the gorse-bushed slopes so you can make as many stops as you wish.   Around the sweeping bend, go over another stile next to a farm gate in the wire fence and keep following the wall.

En route, you will pass several openings in the stone wall which lead into separate fields and one track which turns off into the valley, sharp left.   There are fine views of Encombe House, the stables, the walled garden and the lakes as you enjoy the gentle stroll.   From the turning off, a clear track follows the ridge and, after another stile and gate, it bends round to the right, following the wall to one last stile and gate which leads into Encombe Woods ('The Plantation').   The woodland track passes an opening into a RH field and the drive of "Hill View" house, becoming broken tarmac for a while on the way.   Keep following the track and...... (I know you'll forgive me just this once - but there isn't enough space next to the Stage 1 map for the covering text so read on here whilst referring to the other map).

STAGE 1 (Part)

ENCOMBE WOODS TO KINGSTON

......passing a bank on the LH side, you join a wider "Private Property" track which comes in from your left whilst a Footpath sign points back to Houns Tout.   Follow the dirt track round to the right, past more "Private" tracks to left and right and keep following the main one, again signed for "Kingston" as it turns into a cypress-lined avenue for about 1/2 mile.   This brings you to two short paths on the left - the first into a field and the second into 'The Plantation'" car park .   Immediately after these, you rejoin the lane which led you out of Kingston earlier today.   So go down and catch your bus, or get your car, or have a quick top-up at the "Scott Arms".   It's been a grand Day, hasn't it?   If you didn't go all the way to Kimmeridge, you really ought to come back again and use the Stage maps to make other, shorter circular walks.

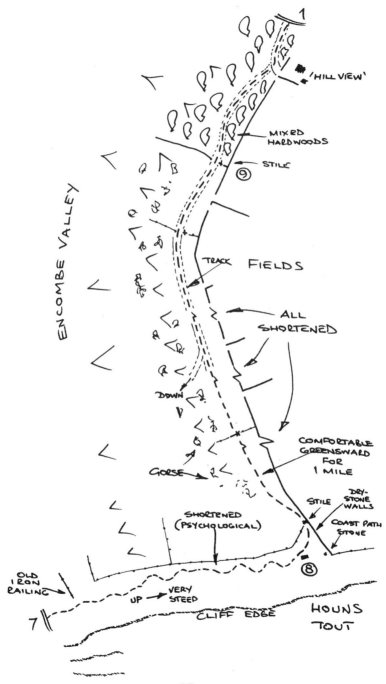

PART SIX - THE MELBURY MEANDER

INTRODUCTION

A truthful title this time, these two walks - which when combined add up to the third walk - really do meander along some of the most peaceful valleys and low chalk hills, through villages remote from the busy main roads and in the grounds of a pair of fine country houses. Both Routes begin in Evershot and Route 1 starts immediately with a walk up the long drive to Melbury Sampford, the manor house of the Strangway family, the Earls of Ilchester who - you will recall from the Abbotsbury Amble - are the lords of Abbotsbury as well. Evershot gets its name from *Eafor's holt*, the wood of the wild boar, and Leland called it "a right humble and poor market town", the market then being held on Saturdays. The manor was bought by Stephen, Earl of Ilchester, in 1761.

The second, and completely charming, stately house is on Route 2 at Chantemarle. Built in the 15thC and added to in the early 17thC, it is now a Police training college but it is very well cared for in its new role.

THE ALTERNATIVES

Our starting point is outside Moorfield House, the Estate Office near the entrance to the Ilchester Estate (Reference ST576047 O S Map No.194) whilst the Rural Bus No 212 from Dorchester and Yeovil stops at School Corner in Evershot.

ROUTE 1: Total distance 6.3/4 miles. This Route starts instantly with a 2 miles stroll through the Park of Melbury Osmond, the seat of the Earls of Ilchester, with its ancient oaks and a herd of deer which dates back at least two hundred years. After visiting the village of Melbury Osmond and its church, the Route crosses farm and meadowland to ancient woods and the hamlet of Melbury Bubb. The historic and tiny church of St Mary the Virgin demands a visit before the journey continues into the bird-filled woods of Bubb Down and then returns along delightful estate tracks through meadows, paddocks and mixed woods to Evershot. The whole circuit is basically not too strenuous and the only steep section is Bubb Down Hill which is about 1:3 for almost 100 feet.

ROUTE 2: Total distance 5.1/4 miles. Starting at the same spot, this Route turns South and heads out of Evershot along fine downland farm trails on the Macmillan Way to the lovely house of Chantmarle and its charming grounds. Then, the Route takes you to the delightful village and lovely St Mary's church of Frome St Quintin. After a glimpse of an Italianate 18thC country house, you return through another farm to Evershot. Although this is an undulating walk, the inclines are mostly gradual and any hills are relatively easy.

ROUTE 3: Total distance 12 miles. When you get back from the fine excursion of Route 1 and you can't bear to wait until another day to finish the Melbury Meander, keep going and follow Route 2. This will complete the Route 3 circuit for you.

STAGE MILEAGES

	STAGE	MILES	TOTAL MILES
ROUTE 1:			
1	Evershot to Melbury Park	1	1
2	Melbury Park to Melbury Osmond	1.50	2.50
3	Melbury Osmond to Church Farm	1.50	4
4	Church Farm to Bubb Down Plantation	1.50	5.50
5	Bubb Down Plantation	1.25	6.75
ROUTE 2:			
6	Evershot to Fortuneswood Farm	1.25	1.25
7	Fortuneswood Farm to Chantmarle	1	2.25
8	Chantmarle to Frome St Quintin	1	3.25
9	Frome St Quintin to Burl Farm	1	4.25
10	Burl Farm to Evershot	1	5.25

ROUTE LAYOUT

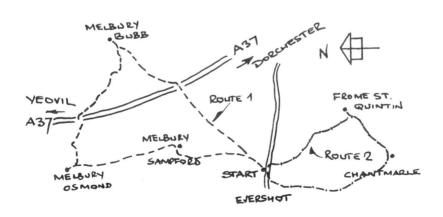

99

STAGE 1

EVERSHOT TO MELBURY PARK

Arriving at the bottom of West Hill, or carefully parking your car on the edge of the road which leads to the Ilchester Estate, set out along the "Private" tarmac drive with the Estate Office drive on your left and the stone "Swiss Cottage" on your right.   You pass a pair of stone mullioned cottages on your left and, after a gate into the LH paddock and a short path up to the high RH field, the grass-verged drive is edged by new framed trees and a high hedge.   The first lane on your right, with a banked LH corner and a RH gate, is the lane down which you will be returning from Route 1 - Stage 5 so make a note of it and don't expect further instructions on how to get back to Evershot from here.   (I *am* getting hard, aren't I?)

Continue up the lane, now with a ditch on your right until, at a LH muddy track, the high RH bank gains a stone wall all the way to the entrance to Melbury Park which you can see up ahead of you.   A tree-filled hedge accompanies you on your left, past a gate and up to the stone Lodge with its ornamented gateposts and a cattle grid across the road.   A short track turns up to the right and a stile leads you safely over the stone boundary wall into the Park.   You now have the prospect of a fine, free walk through the Park with its magnificent old trees, the lovely Melbury Sampford house and its herd of deer.   (This would cost you an arm and a leg if the estate was in the guardianship of the National Trust or English Heritage).   Anyway, up the drive to the brow of the hill, you will find a sunken area on your right which is home to some new trees together with an old pine and an even older beech.   Descending now, a gate in the RH deer fence leads onto a grassy, pine-lined track whilst a turning bears off to the left, signed for "Lodge Farm Only" and "Don't Disturb the Deer".

Walk down to the kissing gate, signed "Public Footpath", next to the cattle grid and enter the part of the Park where you may well encounter the deer.   I once arrived here in early spring just as the deer were being called for feeding.   Most of them were together in the Park area ahead on the left but two enormous, off-white stags with the most incredible antlers suddenly burst from the woods on the right and charged off to get some feed.   They looked more like elk than deer - well, the deer that I was used to meeting in Dorset, anyway.

Carry on down the track, past a right track returning from the valley and a track on your left which leads up to a wooden building.   The surrounding trees are mostly very old oaks, beeches and pines and, as you reach the bottom of the slope, the ground on your right is somewhat marshy.   After some yews on the left, a gravel track turns left, signed "No Right of Way", but keep on up the main driveway..

Through the trees on your right, you can just make out the original sandstone building of Melbury House which, according to Coker, used "3000 loads of free-stone fetched from Hamden quarry, nine miles away".   The manor is in the Domesday Book as *Meleberie*, held by Roger Arundell.   Thomas Strangways and his wife Eleanor came from the Manchester area and their son Henry was the first of the family to come into possession of Melbury Sampford by a will dated 1504.   His son Giles, whilst extending this house, also added the Park and bought the Abbotsbury estates featured in "The Abbotsbury Amble" from Henry VIII for £1096.10.   When you reach the best public viewpoint for the house, the most prominent section is that built by Sir Giles Strangways in the late 17thC whilst its best prospect is that facing East towards the little "ancient but neat pile" of the 15thC church.

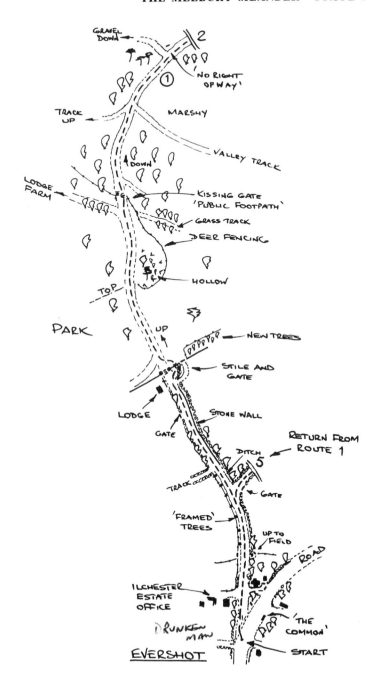

EVERSHOT

MELBURY PARK TO MELBURY OSMOND

Keep on up the drive, passing several turnings to yards and service buildings for the Manor House on your right. There is open parkland on your left, the most likely area for seeing the deer, but keep going as they only usually approach the drive when it's time for feeding. Go through the high kissing gate next to another cattle grid and leave the deer park. You are now entering the equestrian area with wood-fenced paddocks and again with service buildings over on your right.

As the drive turns left by a "Public Footpath" notice, a look back over the double gates which lead onto the lawned front of the house will give you some idea of the magnificence of this noble edifice. The elevation facing you is fine enough but, if you look beyond it, you will be able to make out the original dark sandstone tower of the first Melbury Sampford House. The old building dwarfs the "new" section which faces you whilst, over on its left you will see the little 15thC stone church. The church register dates back to 1580 and the Strangways have been buried here since Dorothy Strangways was the first in 1592.

Now, walk away from the house and past paddocks to left and right. Through the next gate by another cattle grid, the right turning is signed "Private. Keeper Only" so keep straight on, past another paddock on your right and another RH turning. From here, the drive has an avenue of old oak trees and newer trees in frames ready for when the old oaks are no more. Keep straight on down, passing another gravel track turning to your right. This must have been the main drive at one time because the avenue of old oaks follows this direction, not ours, and it leads to the Drive End exit from the Park. The new avenue comes our way though. At the end of our drive, there is another gate and another cattle grid but don't use either. Go over the stile into a small area where there is a handy seat and an opening back into the lane on the other side. Follow the lane down, past the gate into the high, hedged field on the left and past the turn into the old dairy farm yard on your right.

The lane bends left to pass the dairy shed and buildings on your right. A bridleway runs between the thatched cottage facing you and the other pretty cottage on your right but there might not be a sign - unless it's been replaced by now. Follow the lane round a left and a right bend with banked hedges either side and keep descending, past the turn into two cottages down on your left and then with a stream running alongside the LH side of the road. *When you've visited the Church of St Osmund, you'll have to come back here because the next turning on your right leads to Stage 3 and the meander to Melbury Bubb.*

For now, keep on down to the ford which runs between Chapel Cottage on the left and Bridge Farm on the right and use the footbridge on the right to get past it. Begin to ascend with Riverside Cottages on your left and, after a grassy track on your right, Bridge Farm Cottage and a row of fine stone cottages also on your right. After a LH turning and the stone-mullioned Old Post House on your right, you reach the stone-walled garden of the Old Rectory, also on the right, whilst a stone wall leads the road around the top left hand bend. St Osmund's now faces you. It was rebuilt in 1745 by Susanna Strangways Horner in the Georgian style.. "presenting no points of interest. The best part is the handsome monument in various marbles on the South wall of the chancel, describing the piety and munificence of Mrs Strangways Horner and her liberality to the poor" : Rev Hutchins, not me. *Return to Bridge Farm for Stage 3.*

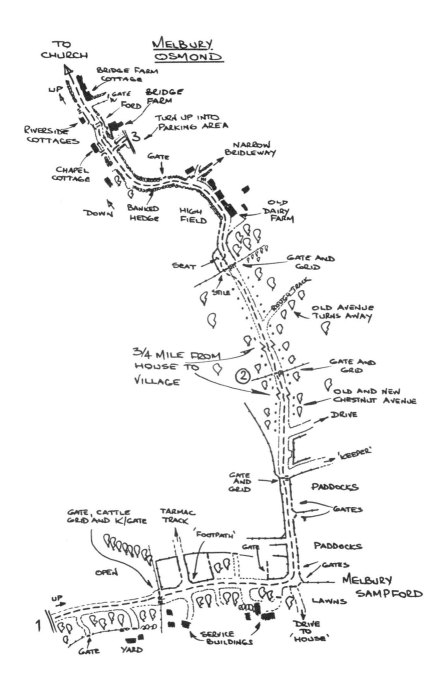

MELBURY OSMOND TO CHURCH FARM

Quietly pass the cottages on your left so that you don't disturb their dog and go through the half-gate at the far end of the communal parking area.   With a paddock on your right, go slightly left past a horse trough and across to the gap in the facing hedge.   Down the short slope, you arrive in the wide avenue and parkland of Melbury Park not far from the Drive End exit.   The stile which you need to leave the Park is not visible from here so I have devised a method for finding it - Follow me.   Turn right, possibly with a faint path, to the corner of the fenced wood over on your right where it meets the drive.   Standing at the corner, you will see that a ditch crosses the grass opposite.   (If you look into the wood, you will see that it emanated from there before the drive was laid across it).   Cross the drive and follow the ditch between the avenue trees down to the low fence where you will find the stile that you need.   Climb over the unmarked stile, cross the handrailed footbridge over the stream and emerge into the uphill field on the other side.   Bear right towards the unmarked first gate in the hedge and go through into the next uphill field.   Follow the LH banked and oak-lined hedge up the ever steeper slope to the top of the field where you will find a gate in the far LH, hedged corner.

After admiring the fine views all around you, go through the gate with a Footpath arrow on the other side and you will find yourself by the entrance to a Car Sales display area on your immediate right.   Carefully cross over the busy A37 Dorchester to Yeovil road and bear left towards "The Welcome Inn".   In the parking area to the right of the inn, you will find two gates.   Ignore the LH, Bridleway-signed gate and go through the RH gate with a signpost for "Footpath. Stockwood Common".   From the gate, the exit stile from this field is about 100 yards to the left along the opposite wire fence, well down from the end of Brickyard Copse which faces you.   The Footpath may not be clear so, if it looks difficult, go anti-clockwise around the edge of the field until you pass the farm gate at the bottom end of the wire fence and you will then find the Footpath-arrowed stile about 15 yards down in the RH hedge.   A double-sleeper bridge spans the stream which runs along the other side of the hedge and it is slippery when wet so be careful.

In this meadow, there is a banked hedge running alongside the stream on your right and a long wood over on your left.   Start off by aiming for the far LH end of the narrow strip of wood and you will go up a long ridge which runs along the field on your way.   When you reach the far corner of the trees and the field widens to your left, stop and look around.   There is an opening in the facing hedge, up on the right, and a farm gate in the adjacent hedge, down on the left.   Go to the gate where you will find a Footpath arrow on a post *on the other side*.   Through this gate, bear right and you will find a Footpath-arrowed stile in the RH hedge, just before a trough near the far corner.   Go over the stile and head towards the first gate in the hedge on your left.

Out of the un-signed gate, turn right onto the lane with a wide verge on the other side and then turn left down the tarmac lane signed for "Church Farm".   There are many barns, sheds and entrances on the left as you begin to descend and ditches on both sides.   You pass a gate in the hedge on your right and, when the hedges give way to wire fences, you will see Church Farmhouse and the adjacent, tiny stone church of St Edwold.   Before the farmhouse, turn left through the Footpath-arrowed gate onto a right-curving track through the field.

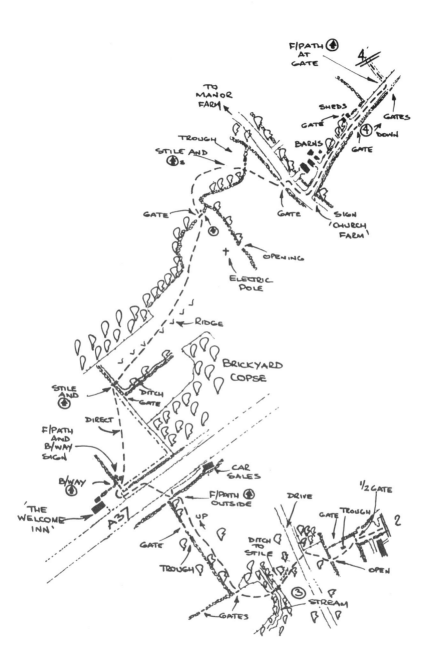

STAGE 4

CHURCH FARM TO BUBB DOWN PLANTATION

Past the footbridge to St Edwold's church, your track crosses the stream and heads up to a fence-enclosed area with a small brick building inside. This was the old path but, as the notice says, "Footpath Closed". The Dorset Council arrows on the fence point you to the diverted path which enters a mixed coppice, pine and oak wood by a Footpath-arrowed stile and a farm gate. Go through onto an ascending chalky clay track which bends right and left on its ascent through the woods. Here, I became an honorary Jack Russell for a whole hour because I was joined by a little terrier who accompanied me all the way to Melbury Bubb and back up to Bubb Down Plantation. I had to send her home because I was going to cross the A37 but I had been delighted to have her company until then. I'm sure it wasn't a privilege reserved just for me, so look out for the little bundle of energy when you pass Church Farm.

At the top of the track you emerge onto Bubb Down Hill at another stile and gate. The yellow arrow points straight up the bowl of the hill with a ridge on your right but I followed the Jack Russell who headed slightly left up the hill and she brought me, impatiently because I couldn't keep up, to the Ordnance Survey 500 ft height mark near the top. From here, you can go down and see the hamlet of Melbury Bubb or go straight across to your right to * for the direct continuation of your walk. It's only 1/4 mile down to Melbury Bubb and the unique church of St Mary the Virgin so it's well worth the detour and this is a meander after all.

Bearing towards the fence on your left, you will find a grassy track which will lead you alongside the LH fence over and down to a farm gate in a shady corner. Go through the unmarked gate and head straight across the sloping field to go anticlockwise around the small brick building in the middle of the field. This is the correct Footpath route on the Definitive Map so go round the shed and then head straight down the hill to the gate by the Dutch barn, after the dead oak tree. Through the gate, keep straight on down to the next gate, again by a barn, and then follow the farm track down through the other barns to the stone wall which surrounds the fine stone-mullioned Manor House. Follow the lane, between the LH hedge and the RH stone wall, round to the right into a wide track area with the white gate of the churchyard facing you and with the road down on your left.

Go through the gate for your visit to the Church of St Mary the Virgin. I said it is unique and, when you see its old solid fuel heater with its fireguard and coal scuttles inside the door - together with its oil wall lights - you'll feel as if you've stepped back a few years. Bubb Down derives its name from Bubba, a Saxon who lived here, and the upside down font in the church was probably once the base of an Anglo-Saxon cross, so a church was here even then. The church was rebuilt in 1474 and the tower from that date was retained when the church was again rebuilt in 1854.

After your visit, retrace you steps up to the O S plinth, then head left across the hill and you'll come to a gate in the wire fence * which leads on to an up and down track in Stock Wood. Follow the track past a RH turn, with a bank on your left and a deep valley on your right, to a gate onto a track which runs down to the A37. Do a left hairpin and go up this adjacent track to a wide grassy area on the right where you will find the first of three Bridleway-arrowed posts. Ignoring the lesser track which runs along the higher slope, follow the long, lower track through Bubb Down Plantation with a strip of wood and a fenced field between you and the A37 down on your right.

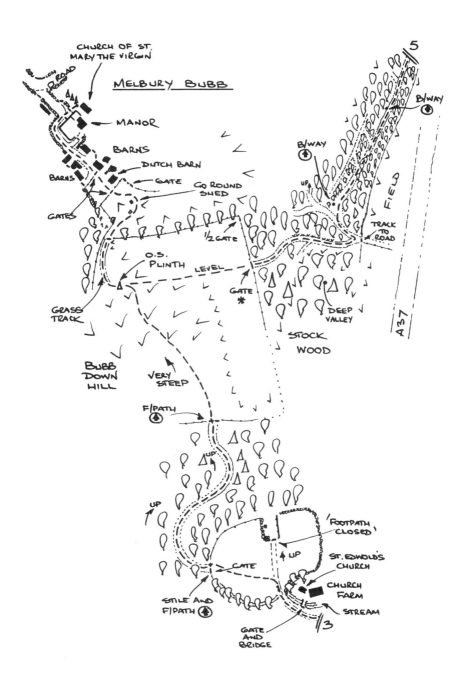

CHURCH OF ST.
MARY THE VIRGIN

MELBURY BUBB

MANOR

BARNS

DUTCH BARN

BARNS

GATE

GO ROUND
SHED

GATES

½ GATE

O.S.
PLINTH

LEVEL

GATE
*

B/WAY

B/WAY

UP

TRACK
TO
ROAD

FIELD

5

B/WAY

A 37

GRASS
TRACK

DEEP
VALLEY

STOCK
WOOD

BUBB
DOWN
HILL

VERY
STEEP

F/PATH

UP

UP

FOOTPATH
CLOSED

UP

ST. EDWOLD'S
CHURCH

GATE

CHURCH
FARM

STILE AND
F/PATH

STREAM

GATE
AND
BRIDGE

3

107

STAGE 5

BUBB DOWN PLANTATION TO EVERSHOT

With a chorus of birds singing their heads off in this old, mixed woodland of beeches and birches, enjoy your slightly ascending stroll along the grassy, chalky track until you come to the third Bridleway-arrowed post just before a left-sweeping bend.   Turn right at the post and descend the steep path through the trees.   With the recent widening of the A37, this new path hasn't been used much but time will improve it. Past another post, you reach a half-gate with fine views to Melbury Sampford house. This brings you out onto the A37, down a bank with a lay-by on your right.

Very, very carefully cross over the road to the milestone on the other side.   The gated and cattle-gridded entrance down on your left is to "Hazel Farm" and the track is now offered as a "Permissive Bridleway" but we'll be better off keeping to the Footpath. Standing by the milestone, marked "Maiden Newton 6 and Yeovil 7", look for a half-gate down on the far side of the newly planted wood - about 5 degrees to the right of the solitary huge old oak down the hill by the T-junction of tracks.   This is still the true Footpath although there may not be any signs so wend your way down to the gate and go through into the vast sloping field beyond.   Walk down the field towards the huge old oak and the track which runs away from it, straight on.

At the bottom, cross the right turning track and follow the gravel track alongside the fenced and ditched edge of the old Hazel Wood on your left.   Go through the gate onto the enclosed track with a wide verge on your right.   Go past the "Private" half-gate into the woods opposite a gate in the RH fence and then past a gated entrance into the woods opposite a stile and horse-jump in the RH fence.

The track now bends right with a dark pine wood on the right and with old oaks on the left.   After a gate into the LH, hedged meadow, there are ditches on both sides which run down to join the stream which comes down the ancient oak-filled meadow and runs away into the wood on your right.   The oaks nearest the stream are cloaked in lovely ferns.   They must be enjoying their abundant water supply.   Rising up out of the valley, the track bends left whilst a more recent track now turns right for a new route on a - as the sign says - "Bridleway to Mel. Osm.".   Turn left and join the long, somewhat ascending, gravel track with the meadow over the hedge on your left and ditches on both sides.   There is always a wood on your right but you will soon have a deep, dark, pine wood on the left to counter the deep, light mixed wood on your right.

Keep on up, past a gate into a paddock and pasture on your left and past a single old yew tree across the RH ditch.   The woods on the right begin to thin out and there are several pines scattered along the RH ditch as you reach a cross-roads of tracks.   There is a gate and a horse-jump on the wide LH corner as the grassier LH track is signed "No Public Right of Way".   The RH track continues through the woods but you keep straight on up, with a ditch before the unfenced wood on your left.   Two tracks run into the LH woods and a track turns into the RH wood near two water tanks - one on the ground and one on a steel tower.   Just past the tanks, after a deep ditch turns into the RH woods, the grass-verged track begins to descend.   After a gate into both left and right fields, the track becomes deeper with harts-tongue ferns in the shady sides and oaks scattered along the high banks.   Just past a huge old beech tree on the left, a driveway turns into a cottage on your left and the track now becomes tarmac with lower banks until you reconnect with the estate road from your starting point at the foot of Evershot.   I said I wouldn't show you the way back from here so - Off you go!

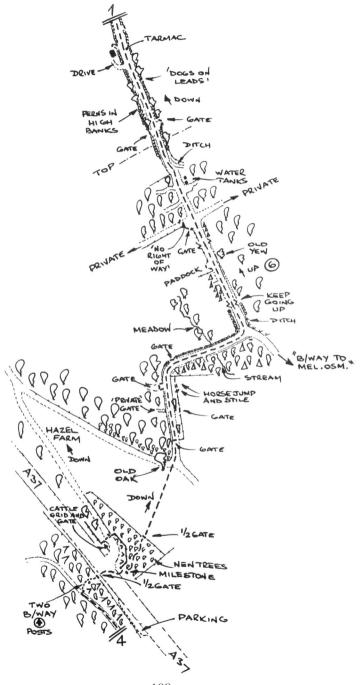

STAGE 6

EVERSHOT TO FORTUNESWOOD FARM

Starting where you started Stage 1, at the foot of Fore Street near the entrance to Melbury Park, follow the pavement up the road past Back Lane on the right with a pair of stone-mullioned cottages over on your left, just before the Village Hall. After a few more cottages on the right, you reach Rectory House where you turn left at School Corner onto "Summer Lane" which is signposted "Cattistock and Maiden Newton". School Corner bus stop stands just up Fore Street on the left, where the raised pavement begins and, if you had the time to visit the top end of Evershot village, the River Frome rises up there, at St John's spring on a wooded ridge.

Past Sticklands C of E Primary School on your left and The Rectory on your right, the road bends right whilst ascending slightly. On the bend, opposite the entrance to Summer Lodge Country House, go through the Footpath-arrowed gate in the LH hedge into the sloping field. There are fine patchwork field views along the valley from here but these get better and better as you progress through this charming landscape which, according to Monica Hutchings in "Inside Dorset".....'is typically Dorset, almost I might say (to the possible comment "what again?") Dorset at its best". Now, get your bearings. Turn up the sloping field, aiming for the gap at the LH end of the top hedge. On the way up, the gap becomes clearer and, after you pass to the right of a hollow near the top of the field, you go through this gap where you will find a Macmillan Way arrow pointing your way along the high slope.

Keep following the banked hedge down, past a track which turns up into the top field (with West Wood Farm over the right horizon), past a trough where the hedge gives way to a new fenced hedge and past a clump of trees on your left. The views are even better as the field levels out and, after a RH gate and stile, you reach the corner gate with another Macmillan Way arrow. At this gate, aim for a spot approx 50 yards to the left of the highest tree on the other side of this wide field (practically straight on), passing a clump of oaks on your left on the way. You will find another Macmillan arrow at the farm gate as you leave the field and join a tarmac drive running down from right to left.

Turn down between the LH verged hedge and the RH fenced field, following the descending drive into a pleasant area shaded with old oaks, now between fences, until a turning runs down into the yard and barns of Fortuneswood Farm. Keep on the main track, past the farmhouse and a row of cottages on your left. The track now climbs up, past another cottage on the RH corner and along high banks to right and left, past a left turning track by a single large oak and up to a right bend into more barns. Don't follow the right bend but bear left here to join another track which runs along the LH wire fence to lead you around to the left side of the large dutch barn. Go through the gate with a Macmillan Way arrow on an adjacent post, where another track comes up from your left, and follow the main track straight on with a hedge on your right.

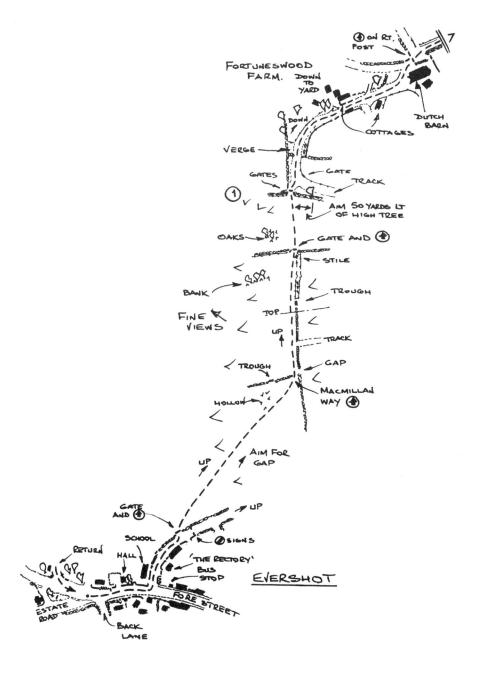

FORTUNESWOOD FARM TO CHANTMARLE

Follow this level track, with the LH field and the RH hedge, to a junction of fields. At the first Macmillan Way arrow, zig-zag slightly right/left, ignoring all other gates or openings, and go through the facing opening (or gate if there is one), again with a Macmillan arrow on the post. Follow the LH wire fence, passing a round trough in this field, until the fence runs out, with a horse jump about 50 yards down on your left. Keep straight on across and down this wide field, aiming for the RH end of the wood down the field ahead of you. As you descend, you will see a stile in a wire fence some way ahead but you have another hedge to pass before you reach it. It's a good direction indicator, though.

At the foot of this field, go through the arrowed gate with the mixed new/old wood on your left and with the hedge wandering off drunkenly on your right. Keep on down and cross the dry gulley to the arrowed stile in the wire fence. From here, look straight ahead and choose a line between the last two electricity poles.

This will bring you to the end of the LH hedge where it turns left onto a grass track. A single old oak stands on your right as the track continues right, in a grassy gulley with a beech wood on its left. You can either follow the track down to your left or come with me on the official Footpath over the stile in the facing hedge. The stile brings you onto the football field of the Police Training College and you now aim for the far LH corner into the beech trees, past the corner flag for the attacking right wing. Go down the path between the trees with garages over on your right and join the descending track from your left. The track now has a high LH bank and a ditch on the right as you meet the tarmac drive with a confirmation Macmillan Bridleway signpost on the RH corner.

All of these modern buildings are training departments for the Police College but, as you follow the drive past the tree shaded lawns and parking areas on your left, the older sandstone buildings on your right are the original Chantmarle. In AD 1211, the 12th year of the reign of King John, Robert Chantmarle held lands here and these were later owned by John Chantmarle whose father had, through marriage, gained Bindon Abbey lands (not far from Wareham). In order to unencumber mortgages which had been raised on Chantmarle, it was sold to John Strode in 1596. It was he who added the superb 'new' house to the original 15thC building, around 1606-12. He then began to build a private chapel which was completed in 1617.

Quietly strolling down the drive, admire the house and gardens and, if you get the chance, look over the wall just past the ornate gates and you'll see the decorative moat, just before the sunken gardens over the fence on your right. Down below you, you'll see the River Frome threading its way through the gardens and under the railway embankment of the Dorchester to Yeovil line. As you cross the railway bridge, with a field on your left and scots pines on your right, the banked drive ahead is a mass of daffodils at the right time of the year. Before you leave Chantmarle, I have heard an apocryphal tale of a local poacher who, with a torch lashed to his rifle, chased a deer one night until it finally ran out into a wide open, grassy area where he was able to get a good shot at it. This wide, grassy area turned out to be the front lawn of Chantmarle and the Police Training College. Unfortunately, my information doesn't extend as far as any repercussions.

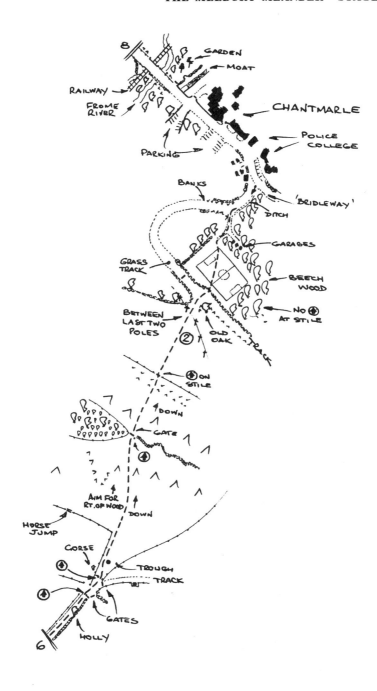

STAGE 8

CHANTMARLE TO FROME ST QUINTIN

Before the iron-fenced banks, turn left through the first Footpath-arrowed gate onto the golf course. On a right bearing from the gate, there is a gable end of a cottage visible above the horizon. Aim right of this cottage and, as you progress across the course, you will see a stile in the facing hedge, next to a holly tree. Go over the arrowed stile into the next field which houses foundations of some demolished buildings. Follow the RH paddock fence to the line of trees ahead of you. The River Frome runs along the margins of the next few fields. Down the dip, you will find an un-arrowed stile and a twin-sleeper bridge across the river. On the other side, bear right, slightly uppish across the marsh grass and away from the riverside trees.

Between the end of the downhill hedge and the end of the uphill fence, you will find an opening. Go through onto the next sloping field and keep high up to brush the hedge as it turns round to the left. Now go over the next un-arrowed stile and aim for the half-gate in the next hedge (this is halfway down from the top hedge). There are farm buildings and a pond down on your right. In this last field, keep straight on down towards the gate in the far LH corner as the LH hedge and fence comes down the hillside to meet it and the stream (river) heads off right to find the valley bottom.

Go through the gate and you will find a Footpath arrow by the road on the other side. This is Frome St Quintin, or Little Frome. In the Domesday Book as *Litel Frome* held by the King, the St Quintin part comes from ancient lords of this manor. Turn left up the road with a high, neatly-trimmed yew (or leylandii) hedge opposite. There is a steeply banked area of trees behind the ivy-clad stone wall on the left bend whilst there are a couple of houses on your right. Then a track turns off right to a cottage on the bend and, immediately after that, a signed grass track leads, between the high LH bank and wooden fence and a RH stone wall, to a gate at its end.

To visit the little church of St Mary, go through the gate and up the field. It dates back to the 12thC and the tower is probably Norman as it has a Norman doorway from the nave. The stone and flint church has additions of the 14thC and 15thC but Hutchins says "it is a small ancient building and contains nothing remarkable". Maybe oil wall lights weren't remarkable in Hutchins' time but they are now. The site is lovely with its bird song and its bench in a sunny spot near the tower from which there are fine views of the village and the fields - which can't have changed much since then. Of course, such things weren't unusual in the Victorian era but these quiet places can bring immense pleasure to the 20th Century soul. Two items struck me as worthy of mention. First, in 1682 Sara Maber married one Thomas Hardy in St Mary's - No, not that Thomas Hardy. Second, in the years between 1418 and 1511, there were nine rectors here, eight of whom were named William (the other one was John Vagg, 1461-1487). Originality wasn't strong in these parts.

After your visit to St Mary's, go back to the road and turn uphill with the stone wall still on your left and with the steep bank on your right. At the top, there is a long brick wall on your right, shielding the Manor House gardens from the outside. As you progress along the road, there are some lovely cottages on your left but always the Manor House wall on your right. You can see the gracious brick and stone building of 1782 through the ornate gates half way along but keep straight on, past Hunters Lodge on the left and gates to right and left, until the road descends between high banked hedges.

STAGE 9

FROME ST QUINTIN TO BURL FARM

With gates into fields on the RH side, the road bends left past a LH cottage and begins to ascend between the LH hedge and the RH high banked hedge.   Still climbing, the road bends right after a house on your left.   Then, after a couple of tree-sheltered houses on your left, the high hedge comes down the slope to join you, with a wide-verged and banked hedge on the left.   After a LH field gate, you arrive at a crossroad of tracks as the road bends right.   The signpost on the RH island confirms directions along the tracks to "Yeovil Road 1/2" and "Evershot 1.1/2".   We're on our way back to Evershot now, sadly, so turn down the gravel track on your left but not before looking over the gate for a lovely retrospective view of Chantmarle.

Enjoying the downhill stroll, the farm which you can see on the slopes ahead of you is Burl Farm, your next immediate target, whilst you can see the West Wood Farm ridge over on your left.   After a low LH ditch, at a low part of the track with a gate in the RH hedge, another grassy track turns down left through a gate.   Now, go up and over a ridge on your rutted, grassy track and you will arrive at an abandoned, ivy-clad cottage on your right with a clump of trees on your left.   Go through the gate into the downhill field and keep straight on, avoiding the electricity pole's support cable en route.   In the bottom RH corner, go over the stile onto the approach to the Yeovil-Dorchester rail track and, as the notice says, "Stop, Look, Listen - Beware of Trains". If all clear, quickly cross the track into the safety of the narrow, fenced enclosure on the other side and go down to another stile into the wooded valley bottom with the young River Frome threading its way from right to left.   Cross the stream where it flows under an oak tree and negotiate the marshy bottom edge of this next uphill field, passing roots or plants of wild iris on the way up.   Don't wander off the narrow path or you might fall into one of the low water tanks.   At the top of the slope, go through the Footpath-arrowed half-gate in the RH fence and wander around the top slope to find your way through the wire fence on the left..

Now, I have had to report problems with the next stage of the official Footpath to Dorset Council because various obstructions have been built across the Path on the Frome St Quintin to Evershot section around Burl Farm.   The Holywell to Evershot section on the other side of Burl Farm is perfectly clear but, to get to it, you have to go through the farmyard which is *not* official Footpath.

I show the route which is the nearest possible to the official Path on the Stage Map as **Route X**. I have walked this route, which should go straight up the hill from this gate, crossing two narrow fields on its way to the clump of trees although the stile is in the wrong place and a slurry pit has been built in the second field.   The route should be reinstated now that the problems have been reported.   So, if it is clear when you arrive, go that way, across the first field, around the slurry pit enclosure and up to the clump of trees in the large open field beyond, passing between the two central oaks in the clump

However, if it is not clear, leave the first field via the farm gate which leads you out onto the track with a banked, low barn on your left and the farmhouse ahead of you, down a little on your right.   Go through the farmyard as a temporary alternative on **Route Y** and join the main gravel track/Footpath which comes up right from Holywell on the far side of Burl Farm.

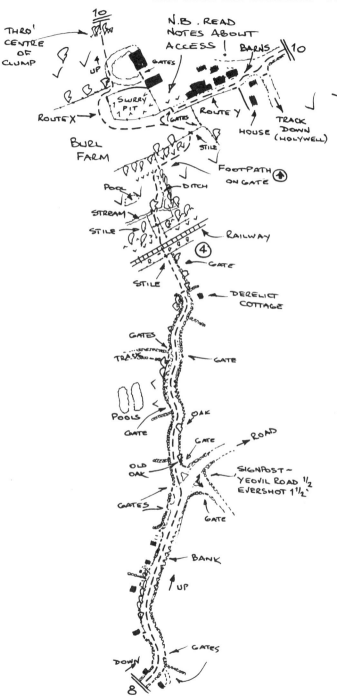

BURL FARM TO EVERSHOT

ROUTE X:
From the twin oaks in the clump, look up the slope and you will see a pair of oaks springing from the same root up on your left and, over the brow of the hill, the top of more oaks. Your route is a line half-way between these two landmarks, straight up. Nearer the top, you will see a hedge facing you with a trough and a gate close to an oak and a holly tree. (Another gate near the corner is just up a bit from your original target oaks). Go through the facing gate into the next field and cross this field, aiming for the far corner (not following the RH hedge to the nearer corner). On your way across, you will make out a trough near the top corner and a gate next to it, by another oak tree. When you get there, go through the gate to meet the enclosed, grassy Holywell track from Burl Farm (and those on Route Y).

ROUTE Y:
Joining the uphill, gravel track, follow it round past a stone and timber barn on the right and with a deep clump of oaks on the left. Past two gates on your right, you arrive at a gate in the top hedge across your track. Through the gate, follow the track as it bends left up and across the field and arrives at another gate in the far corner. Lo and behold, there is a Footpath arrow on this gate - the first since the half-gate after the railway line. Go through the gate and follow the track between the LH hedge and the RH wire fence to a junction of gates at the end (where Route X joins you through the first LH gate).

Now, all being equal, it's plain sailing back to Evershot from here. Keep straight on along the grassy track near the LH banked hedge, past a gate and descending to another LH gate and a Footpath-arrowed gate in the far corner. Go through this hedge gate and keep straight on across the open, sloping field to a gap in the opposite banked hedge, just below a short oak. Still downish, go straight across to a bent oak tree where you will find an arrowed half-gate in the next hedge and fence.

In this last field, you will see a single oak tree ahead of you and clumps of bushes and trees running along the bottom left of the sloping field. Turn half down the slope and aim for a stile next to a holly tree. On the way down, for a correct line, you shouldn't come any closer than 30 yards to that oak tree. Arriving at the Footpath-arrowed stile, go over it and up and over a bushed bank to drop down to stream (Yes, the young River Frome again). Cross the stream by the simple bridge and go up and over another bank to cross a ditch, finally ascending to the tarmac track with thin bushes and poplars on the other side. Turn right onto the track and follow it alongside the hazel and willow clad stream, past a gate where the stream runs under the track and into an open area where there is a thatched stable block and some garages. On the other side of the stream, now on your left, is the old Common Farm - or rather *was* the old Common Farm as plans are being considered (or have already been passed) for the building of 21 dwellings - or there are 21 dwellings on the other side of the stream. There, I think that covers all possibilities (other than the plans being rejected, which I doubt) so a revision to "The Melbury Meander" shouldn't be necessary just yet.

Anyway, keep straight on out of the track and into "The Common", just opposite your starting point with "Swiss Cottage" on your right and the start of Route 1.

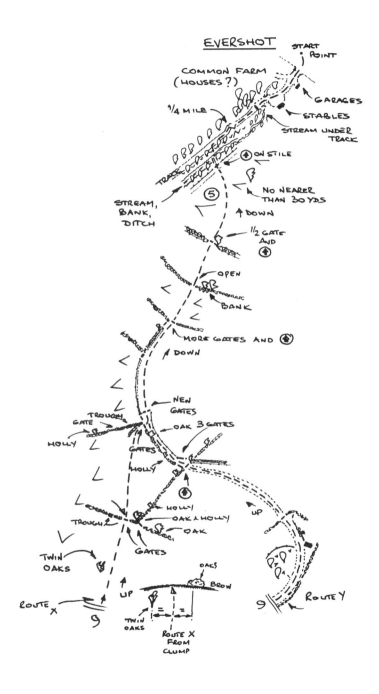

PART SEVEN - THE BOTTLEBUSH ROUND

INTRODUCTION

I couldn't find any words associated with walking which begin with a B so we might as well get straight on with the "Round". This strange, tumuli-bedecked and Roman road-bisected, upland area of deepest Dorset has long fascinated me. It has been the subject of my earlier long-distance walk guide *"The Cranborne Chase Path"* but I have been drawn back to its mysterious footpaths and bridleways many times. This is an ancient forest, much patronized by Royalty in Tudor and Jacobean times and this, together with its avoidance by the builders of the Great Western Turnpike in the late 18th Century, explains why it has remained undeveloped. This is the land of Bronze and Iron-age settlements and it has been the scene of many conflicts between these early settlers and the invaders who included the Roman hordes, the Saxons and the Normans. Since then, there have been conflicts on a lesser scale, although no less bloody, between poachers and Chase wardens. So, drink in the atmosphere and *go quietly!* - You never know what you might see if you travel circumspectly.

The alternative Routes, which are mostly along easy farm tracks and paths, all begin with the shortest walk so that extensions from it are easier to follow and, when you turn off to the longer alternatives, I will tell you what you can expect to come across along the way. Of course, whichever option you choose, you won't cover all of the sections in one Day (unless you're a fast walker) so if, like me, you come to love Cranborne Chase, you can come back and enjoy walking all of the mapped stages.

Because of its escape from development, Cranborne Chase doesn't have all of the facilities which you may expect, such as Pubs, shops and supermarkets except - on a gentle scale - in Cranborne itself. So pack a good lunch in your backpack, lace up your walking boots and go and have a fine day's hiking over some of the best chalk downs and dairy and arable farmland anywhere in the County - or in the country.

By the way, there aren't that many buses to get you to the Squirrels Corner start but Wilts and Dorset buses Nos. 184 and 185, together with the Rural Services 323 and 400, will deliver you to Handley Cross roundabout just 1/2 mile away. There are also Rural Buses to Cranborne village, Nos. 300, 302 and 303, which may be useful.

THE ALTERNATIVES

Starting at the parking area at Squirrels Corner on the B3081 (Reference SU025153 on O S Map No. 184), these round walks cover between 5.1/4 and 13.1/2 miles, depending on which option you choose. **Options 1, 2, 3 and 5 all begin at Route 1 - Stage 1 so you can't get lost and Option 4 has its own start at Route 4 - Stage 1.** Simple, isn't it?.

ROUTE 1: Total distance 5.1/4 miles - This shorter of the four Routes takes you along Ackling Dyke to a unique series of tumuli, up to Penbury Knoll hill fort, past the source of the River Crane and back to Squirrels Corner along some fine tracks and a Drove Road, field footpaths and open downland.

ROUTE 2: Total distance 6 miles - An additional 3/4 mile to Route 1 includes a slightly longer section of the Drove Road, a visit to Cranborne Farm and a chance to ford the River Crane.

ROUTE 3: Total distance 8 miles - The extra 2 miles added to Route 2 takes you all the way into Cranborne where you can visit the Manor House gardens and the Church and learn something of the history of the centre of this Royal Chase.

ROUTE 4: Total distance 5.1/2 miles - This Route stays South of the B3081 and includes a fine walk along farm tracks, through woodlands, across the Monkton-up-Wimborne road and over the River Allen to Harley Wood. It includes a more shady stretch of the Ackling Dyke and it can be added conveniently to any of the other Routes to make an interesting extension if you feel like staying out a little longer when you get back to Squirrels Corner.

ROUTE 5: Total distance 13.1/2 miles - This is the "total" Route, being formed from the outer edge of the whole circuit to make the longest possible alternative Just by following Route 3, you will arrive back at Squirrels Corner after 8 glorious miles and then you can carry on with Route 4 for another 5.1/2 miles. This way, - after a refuelling stop at Squirrels Corner - you get to see the best of this area all at once - and 13.1/2 miles isn't that far really, is it?

STAGE MILEAGE TABLES

Parking is available at Squirrels Corner and along the wide verges of the B3081. Also in Cranborne Car Park and Pentridge (with consideration). As I have already mentioned, buses are available at Handley Cross Roundabout and also at the Pentridge village turn-off from the A354. Buses are Wilts and Dorset's 184 and 185 and Local bus services 323 and 400. Buses to Cranborne village are few but Rural Nos. 300, 302 and 303 may be useful. Oh, and you'll need O S Map No. 195 as well.

STAGE	MILES	TOTAL MILES
ROUTE 1: 13/9/02 (BEAUTIFUL WARM DAY).		
1.1 Squirrels Corner only	0	
1.2 Squirrels Corner to Bottlebush	1.25	1.25
1.3 Bottlebush Down to Cursus Gate	1	2.25
1.4 Cursus Gate to Pentridge Hill ✓	.75	3
1.5 Pentridge Hill to Bowldish Pond	1.50	4.50
1.6 Bowldish Pond to Squirrels Corner	.75	**5.25**
ROUTE 2: 15/9/02		
1.1 - 1.4 as Route 1 to Pentridge Hill	3	3
1.5 Pentridge Hill to Drove Road	.75	3.75
2.1 Drove Road to Cranborne Dairy Farm	.75	4.50
3.3 Cranborne Farm to Squirrels Corner ✓		
(using the last 1/4 mile of 1.6)	1.50	**6**

ROUTE 3: ١٣/٩/٠٢

1.1 - 1.4 as Route 1 to Pentridge Hill	3	3
1.5 Pentridge Hill to Drove Road	.75	3.75
3.1 Drove Road to Cranborne	1.25	5
3.2 Cranborne to Cranborne Dairy Farm	1.50	6.50
3.3 Cranborne Farm to Squirrels Corner (using the last 1/4 mile of 1.6)	1.50	8

ROUTE 4:

4.1 Squirrels Corner to Monkton Up Wimborne	1.25	1.25
4.2 Monkton Up Wimborne to Harley Wood	1.25	2.50
4.3 Harley Wood to Bottlebush Down	2	4.50
4.4 Bottlebush Down to Squirrels Corner (using 1.2 and 1.1 in reverse)	1	**5.50**

ROUTE 5:

1.1 - 3.3 Returning to Squirrels Corner after completing Route 3 (using the last 1/4 mile of 1.6)		8
4.1 - 4.4 (i.e. all of Route 4)	5.50	**13.50**

ROUTE LAYOUT

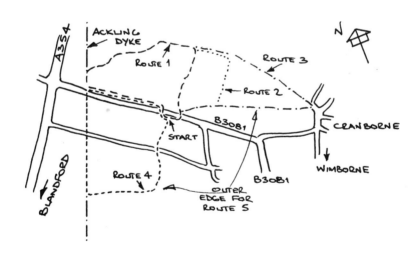

122

ROUTE 1 - STAGE 1

SQUIRRELS CORNER

Routes 2 and 3 start here as well, don't forget - and **Route 5** if you've already decided to go all the way.

Having parked and secured your car, having been dropped off in the parking area amongst the trees on the South side of the B3081 at Squirrels Corner (Reference SU025153 on O S Map No. 184 to repeat myself) or having dismissed your bus driver, turn to face the road and go up the track on your left, nearest to and parallel with the road, for a short distance. When you reach the corner of a wire fenced area, very carefully cross over the road from a very wide verge on this side to an equally wide verge on the other side - only because the views will be better and the track will be firmer in a few moments.

That's all there is for you on Stage 1 because most of this map is concerned with making sure you're starting at the right place. So, when you're safely on the other side, all turn to Route 1 - Stage 2.

ROUTE 1 - STAGE 1

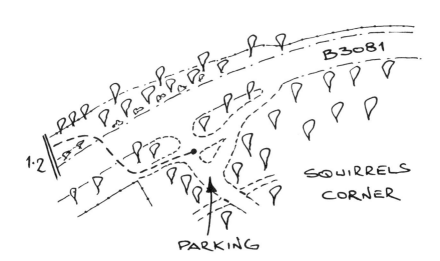

ROUTE 1 - STAGE 2

SQUIRRELS CORNER TO BOTTLEBUSH DOWN

As you walk along this very wide verge, you should find that the grass has been mowed quite short and, on this side, there is ample parking for a very long stretch between the roadside and the tree-lined wire fence on your right.   After a pair of stump-protected tumuli, one either side of the road, an opening in the RH fence at the junction of two fields gives a view of the line of the Dorset Cursus - a low bank, similar to the Ackling Dyke which you will soon be joining. The line actually runs along the RH edge of the wood which you can see at the end of the wire fence.

The Dorset Cursus was a ceremonial route of indeterminate origin, with parallel banks about 1/4 mile apart, which strides across Bottlebush Down from Gussage Hill to Martin Down - although very little is visible from the ground. The Romans weren't impressed.   They cut straight across it with their Ackling Dyke about 1 mile South-West of here (much the same as the Turnpike builders built over the Ackling Dyke down in the distance on your right where the Dyke runs into, and becomes, the A354).

Anyway, keep straight on and you will soon arrive at a solitary apple tree and the Footpath-arrowed stile onto the Ackling Dyke on your right. Climb over the stile onto the top of Ackling Dyke and follow the faint path as it zig-zags through some sparse hawthorn bushes on a descending slope. There is a grassy track and a banked field on your right and a wide, lower field on your left. At a cutting near the bottom of the sloping path, come down off the Dyke and join the track along the edge of the, now unfenced, RH field.

Ackling Dyke Stile, Bottlebush Down. Page 124

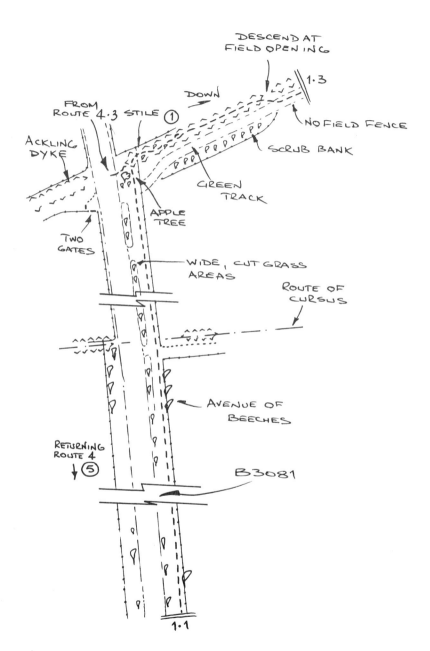

DESCEND AT
FIELD OPENING

DOWN

1.3

FROM
ROUTE 4.3 STILE ①

NO FIELD FENCE

ACKLING
DYKE

SCRUB BANK

③

GREEN
TRACK

APPLE
TREE

TWO
GATES

WIDE, CUT GRASS
AREAS

ROUTE OF
CURSUS

AVENUE OF
BEECHES

RETURNING
ROUTE 4

↓ ⑤

B3081

1.1

BOTTLEBUSH DOWN TO CURSUS GATE

At the corner of the mixed beech and pine wood, where a grassy track turns off alongside the woods to your right, go back onto the top of the faint Dyke where Footpath arrows point backwards and onwards.   After a few yards, with vague tracks nearby on your left, next to a horse-jump in the wire fence, go over a stile into the next field.   Here, tumuli and other earthworks abound - so much so that, whilst adjoining fields are always planted, this field is left untouched.

This famous assemblage of disc and bowl barrows is listed by L V Grinsell as "Oakley Down, Wimborne St Giles - the finest barrows of their kind" but Oakley Down is the other side of the A354 over on your left and Wimborne St Giles is a good 3 miles away South-East from here.

Where a track comes through the farm gate from the field on your right and cuts across your path to disappear into the tumuli field, an intriguing earthwork presents itself. Basically, it is a 216 ft diameter disc barrow with two tumps (internal mounds) inside it and with two cuttings through it.   In true road builders style, the Romans cut straight into the edge of this ancient monument rather than bend the Ackling Dyke a few feet.   As Heywood Sumner says in his 1913 treatise "Both roads (this and the A354) cut into the barrow circles and both thus express a silent disregard for departed glory".   When the barrows in this field were excavated in Victorian times, nearly every one contained a cremation urn, amber beads and some bronze artefacts.

Now, back on top of the Dyke, go over the stile next to the horse-jump into the next RH field and, within a few yards, come down off the rapidly deteriorating Dyke towards the equally rapidly deteriorating wire fence.   With the Dyke temporarily reduced to a series of shallow bumps and hollows, go through the gate into the RH field, next to a pair of horse-jumps and two posts with Bridleway arrows.

In this next, uphill, field, follow the edge of the woods on your right ('Salisbury Plantation' which was originally planted in 1939) and leave the Ackling Dyke - for now, at least.   After a gate into the woods on the RH side, the fence bears slightly right so follow the fence, past a gate into the woods and around two more corners, until you arrive at the wide gateway into the next field, with a cattle trough behind the fence on your left.

The final, short section of wire fence on your right, together with the far edge of Salisbury Plantation, exactly follows the line of the Dorset Cursus so that, as you go through the gateway, you cross its Eastern flank on the brow of this hill.

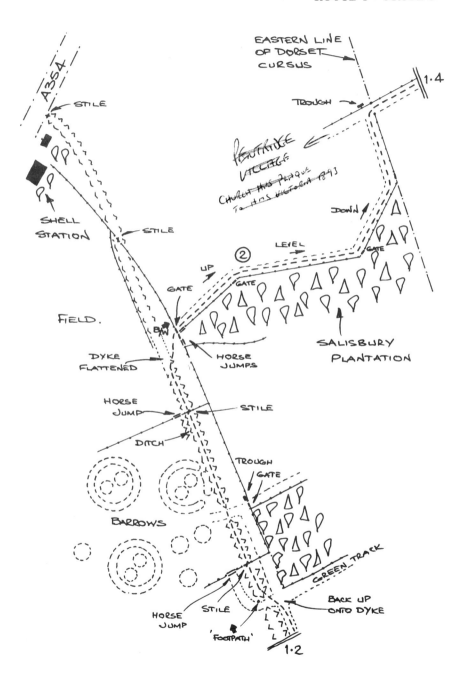

EASTERN LINE
OF DORSET
CURSUS

1·4

A354

STILE

TROUGH

SHELL
STATION

STILE

PENITATIVE
VILLAGE
CHURCH HAS PLAQUE
TO HMS VICTORIA 1843

DOWN

LEVEL

②

UP

GATE

GATE

GATE

FIELD.

B/W

DYKE
FLATTENED

HORSE
JUMPS

SALISBURY
PLANTATION

HORSE
JUMP

STILE

DITCH

TROUGH

GATE

BARROWS

GREEN TRACK

BACK UP
ONTO DYKE

HORSE
JUMP

STILE

'FOOTPATH'

1·2

CURSUS GATE TO PENTRIDGE HILL

Follow the descending track on the LH side of this field, with good views to Pentridge village and church on your left. Look across to your right for views into the valley which leads up to the B3081 and straight ahead for views of Pentridge Hill (which you will soon be ascending). Below you on your left, a long line of tall pines strides off into Pentridge.

At the bottom of this field, a track turns off alongside the RH hedge but your route goes past the start of that line of pines, past an opening back on the left into a field and round to a boggy bit of track (unless it's high summer when you walk this Route). This is where the Pentridge village valley bottom drains towards the headwaters of the River Crane. I hope it's dry and set hard when you arrive. After the Bridleway arrow on a post on your right, by a gate into the valley bottom, the track bears off to the left, between hedges, to Pentridge.

In the Domesday Book, Pentridge is listed as *"Pentric"* - belonging to the Church of Glastonbury. The name is derived from the British 'pen', a head or chief part and 'ridge', as of a hill.

Don't go that way, though. Turn right, through twin gates by a Bridleway arrow, and follow the uphill, deeply rutted track with grass up the middle, round the LH bend with an open field on your right. As you follow the sunken track, on a seemingly ever-upward slope, you go past a dug-out silage pit below you on your right and then you pass a pair of heavy gate posts with no gates.

With the track still deeply sunken, pass a horse-jump in the fence on your right and a few scrubby bushes on both sides. Two bushes up ahead of you mark where the last gate crosses this track, next to another horse-jump in the wire fence which runs across the lower slopes of Pentridge Hill. Go through the gate onto the grazing slopes of the Hill where you will find tractor tracks fading into the grass. Keep on, following the line of the fence on your right, past a hawthorn bush, into and out of a dip which passes through the fence, past a three-barred horse-jump and up to a farm gate at the top end of the fence. I know I said that Penbury Knoll hill fort was on this Route. Well, it is, if you turn left here and wander over the top slopes of the hill, and through the small gate into the pine woods. The slopes of the earthworks are clearly visible on the far side of Pentridge Hill and are well worth a picnic stop. Come back to this gate, with the Bridleway arrows, when you've finished exploring and go through into a wide, well horse-trodden area with small trees on either side.

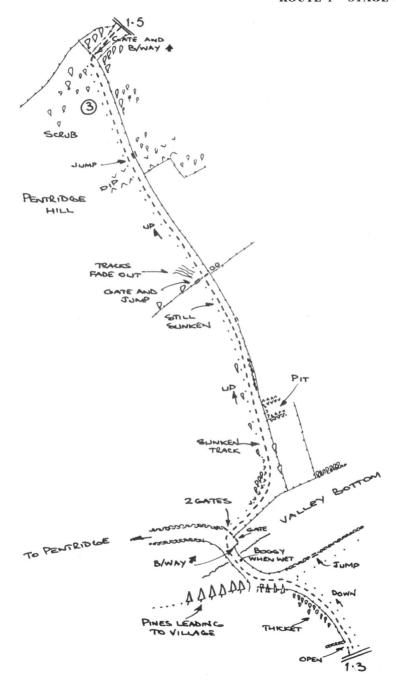

1·5

GATE AND
B/WAY

③

SCRUB

JUMP

DIP

PENTRIDGE
HILL

UP

TRACKS
FADE OUT

GATE AND
JUMP

STILL
SUNKEN

PIT

UP

SUNKEN
TRACK

2 GATES

VALLEY BOTTOM

TO PENTRIDGE

GATE

B/WAY

BOGGY
WHEN WET

JUMP

DOWN

PINES LEADING
TO VILLAGE

THICKET

OPEN

1·3

129

ROUTE 1 - STAGE 5

PENTRIDGE HILL TO DROVE ROAD AND BOWLDISH POND

Make sure that you don't bear off to the right here because that particular track only leads to a "Private Wood". Keep to the clear track, past the Bridleway arrow on the wire fence corner post and between banks for a while. At first, the track descends slightly with a hedge on your left and an open field on your right. Behind the hedge there are several enclosed clumps of trees, presumably to protect them from grazing herds of cattle. A slight rise is soon followed by another descent with grass up the middle of the track. Then, after a gate in the LH hedge, the Bridleway rises again to meet a pair of farm gates either side of a stile on your right.

AND NOW, IT'S DECISION TIME - DO YOU TAKE THE SHORTEST WAY BACK OR ADD ANOTHER 3/4 OR 2.3/4 MILES TO THE STROLL BACK TO YOUR CAR?

We'll take the short route first and, when I've taken Route 1 walkers to Bowldish Pond and dropped them back at Squirrels Corner, I'll come back and find you. Oh, alright then.

ROUTE 2: Turn to Route 2 - Stage 1
ROUTE 3: Turn to Route 3 - Stage 1.

ROUTE 1:

Now, all you Route 1 walkers, turn off here. Over this stile, you are in a very long field, with a wire fence and a recently planted hedge on your right and a steady climb ahead of you. Fortunately, there is a very wide, grassy path specially for you all the way up and over the brow of the hill and, if you feel like a rest on the way up, there are lovely views behind you down into the valley of Toby's Bottom on the right and far beyond. Anyway, when you reach the end of the field, with a wire fence facing you, there is a farm gate on your right with a Footpath-arrowed stile on its left. Go over this stile, facing Blackbush Down woods, and immediately turn left up the bank onto a farm track which leads to the next fence with another stile in it. Go over this next stile and join the downhill track...

In the shade of the older bushes at the side of this track, I once disturbed a sleeping fallow deer. It's amazing how quickly they come round. He was up and away almost before I'd noticed him. It takes me a lot longer than that to become active after I wake up.

Anyway, keep on down the footpath, with varying hedges, fences and hawthorns on your left, past a turning to a pair of farm gates, again on your left, and down to a small personnel gate with a Footpath arrow on it. Through the gate, join the downward track, bearing left at first. The RH direction is clearly signed "No Right Of Way".

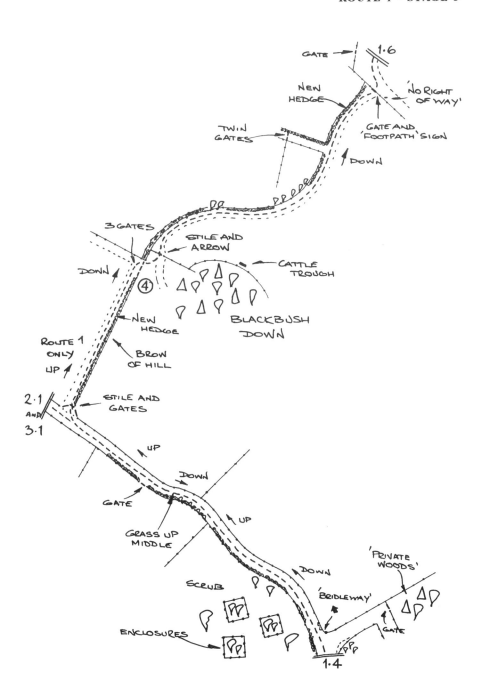

GATE → 1·6

NEW HEDGE

'NO RIGHT OF WAY'

TWIN GATES

GATE AND 'FOOTPATH' SIGN

↑ DOWN

3 GATES

STILE AND ARROW

CATTLE TROUGH

DOWN ↗

④

NEW HEDGE

BLACKBUSH DOWN

ROUTE 1 ONLY UP ↑

BROW OF HILL

2·1 AND 3·1

STILE AND GATES

↑ UP

DOWN →

GATE

↑ UP

GRASS UP MIDDLE

'PRIVATE WOODS'

DOWN

SCRUB

'BRIDLEWAY'

GATE

ENCLOSURES →

1·4

131

ROUTE 1 - STAGE 6

BOWLDISH POND TO SQUIRRELS CORNER

ROUTES 2 AND 3:
You only need the last part of this Stage to show you the road back to Squirrels Corner, so scan down to the penultimate paragraph.

ROUTE 1:
Keep following the track with the open field on your right and with a gate on your left just before an open area with Bowldish Pond beyond some scrubby bushes on your left and a steep bank on your right.   If you follow the edge of the embankment, you will come to a brick footbridge, between trees, over a small stream.   This is preferred because the main track descends into a ford which can be particularly boggy after wet weather.

These are the upper reaches of the River Crane, the stream which gives Cranborne its name and which starts at the foot of Pentridge Hill where you met a boggy patch by the line of pines running into Pentridge village.   Eventually, when it has grown a bit bigger, it runs into the River Stour and the English Channel via Christchurch Harbour.   Now, emerging from the line of trees, keep straight on, past two farm gates and a smaller gate in the wire fence on your left and with a vast, open field on your right

Keep on up this chalky track, soon with grass up the middle, to a conglomeration of gates at the top.   There are twin farm gates on your left and twin farm gates across your path.   Go over the stile with the handpost on the right of the facing gates into a wide area before the B3081.   The small gate on the left leads down to Cranborne village and it is from here that Routes 2 and 3 walkers will be joining you for the last step to Squirrels Corner.

ROUTES 1, 2 AND 3:
All together now, carefully cross over the road to the high grass verge on the other side.   The grass will probably be quite high and soft but stay with it.   It's safer than walking along the road and the more walkers use this verge, the firmer it will become. So, consider yourself a pioneer and trail blazer.   There is a field at first behind the hedge on your left but this soon gives way to a mixed pine and deciduous wood.   The views over the fields on your right are extensive and you can see back to where you reached the Cursus gate earlier today.

Keep on the verge, past a wooden barrier with a "Private. Keep Out" sign in the woods, until you arrive at the vehicle entrance onto the car parking area where you started the walk.

I hope you enjoyed the excursion today.   And don't forget, there are several more walks starting from here for other days and, if you would like to visit Cranborne, you could start there and use Route 3 and Stages 1.6 and 1.5 in reverse to make another most enjoyable circular walk without going onto the B3081 at all.

Route 4 will take you South of the B3081 into completely different country where you will hear of a strange happening and find out about a local prediction of Armageddon - Oh, and it's lovely countryside and farmland as well.

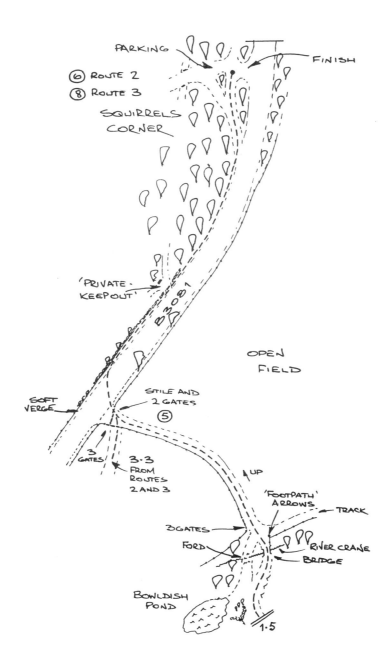

PARKING

FINISH

⑥ ROUTE 2
⑧ ROUTE 3

SQUIRRELS
CORNER

'PRIVATE·
KEEP OUT'

B3081

OPEN
FIELD

SOFT
VERGE

STILE AND
2 GATES
⑤

3
GATES

3·3
FROM
ROUTES
2 AND 3

UP

'FOOTPATH'
ARROWS — TRACK

3 GATES

RIVER CRANE

FORD

BRIDGE

BOWLDISH
POND

1·5

133

ROUTE 2 - STAGE 1

DROVE ROAD TO CRANBORNE DAIRY FARM

Leaving the Route 1 walkers to return to Squirrels Corner, keep straight on up the track which immediately opens out to a very wide area with hawthorn bushes in the grassy bank on your right. The track veers round to the left and drops slightly to a junction. On the RH corner, there is a very comfortable grassy bank where you can sit and enjoy the views down into the valley of Toby's Bottom. There is a footpath down through those fields beyond the gate on your left and a Bridleway, which is also the Jubilee Trail, turns off to the right.

This Bridleway takes you back, via Cranborne Dairy Farm (where you could profitably use a couple of plastic bags), to Squirrels Corner whilst the track straight on is the Route 3 track which goes to Cranborne village and comes back via the same farm - but it is 2 miles longer.

The Route 3 walkers have already decided to go straight on and they are on a different map to you already, so forget them and turn right up this Bridleway, past the corner gate and keep straight on, with a wire fence on your right and with grass up the middle. Beginning to drop down now, a Footpath-signed gate crosses the track and another gate on your right with a "No Right of Way" sign heralds the start of a section of track which is alive with flocks of Peacock and Speckled Wood butterflies in the height of summer. There remains an old, high hedge on your left and a mix of new and old bushes and a wire fence on your right. There is a good view across the field to Blackbush Down woods over on your right.

Still descending, go past a cattle trough in the field on your right and another signed gate across your path - and yet another gate across your path, . Very soon, you will reach a pair of gates on the left and two gates on your right which lead into a field. Next to them, there is a small gate with a Footpath arrow and a "Please Shut the Gate" sign on the adjacent post.

Here, you join the Route 3 walkers on their return from Cranborne so turn to Route 3 - Stage 3 as this is everybody's way back to Squirrels Corner.

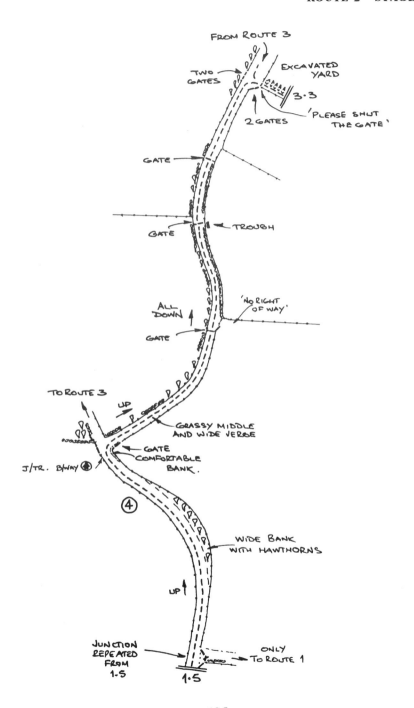

FROM ROUTE 3

TWO GATES

EXCAVATED YARD

3·3

'PLEASE SHUT THE GATE'

2 GATES

GATE

GATE ← TROUGH

'NO RIGHT OF WAY'

ALL DOWN ↑

GATE

TO ROUTE 3

UP →

GRASSY MIDDLE AND WIDE VERGE

GATE COMFORTABLE BANK.

J/TR. B/WAY ④

④

WIDE BANK WITH HAWTHORNS

UP ↑

JUNCTION REPEATED FROM 1·5

ONLY TO ROUTE 1

1·5

ROUTE 3 - STAGE 1

DROVE ROAD TO CRANBORNE

Leaving the Route 1 walkers to return to Squirrels Corner, keep straight on up the track which immediately opens out to a very wide area with hawthorn bushes in the grassy bank on your right. The track veers round to the left and drops slightly to a junction. On the RH corner, there is a very comfortable grassy bank where you can sit and enjoy the views down into the valley of Toby's Bottom. There is a Footpath down through the fields beyond the gate on your left whilst the "Jubilee Trail" signed Bridleway turns off right to take the Route 2 walkers back, via Cranborne Dairy Farm, to Squirrels Corner without visiting Cranborne. Don't worry about them. They're on a different map already.

Keep straight on, between the higher fenced field on your right and the hedge on a dipping fence on your left. This Bridleway rises a little and, after a higher patch and a single beech tree on the right, the track widens out and levels. The RH fence gives way to a banked hedge and an entrance into the RH field has been replaced by a wire barrier. As the RH, banked hedge becomes infiltrated by holly bushes, the wide grassy track continues to rise slightly and you reach an opening into an old beech wood on a low hill on the left. There are several yew trees along the LH edge of the track now and, over the RH hedge, the fields drop down into a winding valley.

Here, with old man's beard (wild clematis) in the LH hedge, the track is not so wide and opposing openings lead into the LH trees and the level RH field respectively. You now begin to descend as the banked track wends its way, past holly bushes on the left and a wire-fenced gap on the right, to a Bridleway-arrowed gate across the track where you pass around its LH end. After the house on your left, there is a fine twin-gabled, red brick house with a double drive, just before a LH field gate, and a wide track/Bridleway emerges through a pair of gates on your right.

Still descending, with banked hedges either side, you arrive at a junction with the ancient Cranborne to Martin and Toyd Down road which once led all the way to Salisbury before being superseded by the Great Western Turnpike (the A354). The signpost on the corner verge indicates the ways to "Boveridge 1.1/2 and Martin 4.3/4" whilst it confirms that you are emerging from the "Bridleway to Pentridge". Keep to the RH banked hedge with a high yew hedge on the LH side of the road and, in a few yards, before the first house in Cranborne (for this is where you are), there is a "Salisbury Street" plaque on the RH brick wall. If you pass this sign, you've gone too far. You should turn right alongside the garden wall, which has a faint yellow arrow painted on its corner, and follow the path to the kissing gate at the top end with a field on your right and a tile-topped, rendered wall on your left.

Go through the gate and turn left to keep the line of successive garden walls on your left. Go through the gate to the left of the avenue of trees which lead down to Cranborne Manor House and visit Cranborne by turning to Route 3 - Stage 2.

Before you leave Cranborne, it would be a good idea to take a couple of plastic carrier bags with you ready for Stage 3. Have a sneaky look at Route 3 - Stage 3 if you don't like surprises.

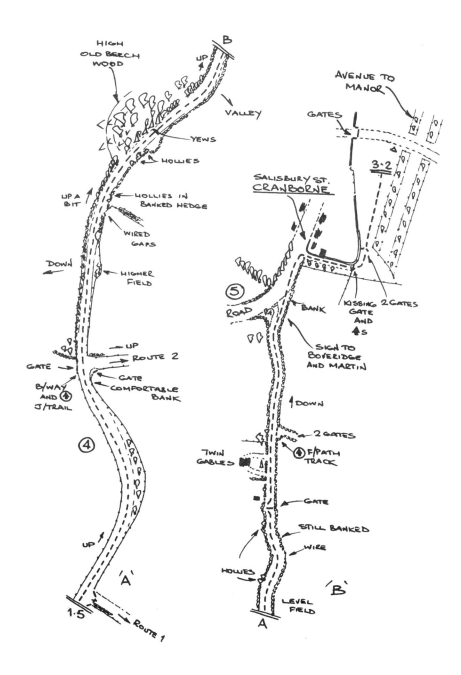

CRANBORNE TO CRANBORNE DAIRY FARM

Before 1066, there was a Benedictine Abbey here but Abbot Giraldus of Cranborne, founded another Abbey in Tewkesbury in 1091 and, eleven years later, he and the 57 monks removed to Tewkesbury. This resulted in Cranborne Abbey being demoted to a Priory or Cell of Tewkesbury and so it remained until it was dissolved in 1540.

Cranborne's history is best documented in Wake-Smart's "Chronicle of Cranborne and the Cranborne Chase" but much more readably in Desmond Hawkins "Cranborne Chase". The Chase Court was held here, mainly because Robert Cecil, 1st Earl of Salisbury and Queen Elizabeth's First Secretary, later James I's Lord Treasurer, lived in Cranborne Manor House (as do his descendants to this day) and the Court was conveniently held there. Cranborne had enjoyed a prime position on the road from Poole to Salisbury but the Great Western Turnpike, which was begun in 1755, passed it by and Cranborne's importance was ended. The market house was demolished in 1828. Cranborne Chase's royal hunting connections date back to King John who hunted here on fourteen occasions, finally building a hunting lodge where now stands the Manor House. Robert Cecil entertained James I on his many hunting trips and, after Cecil's death in 1612, James returned here many times between 1615 and 1623. Following damage to the house during the Civil War, when the Cecils supported Parliament, the house was unoccupied for many years but, after a 100 year period of use as farmhouses, it was renovated by the 2nd Earl of Salisbury in 1863 (the title of Earl of Salisbury having been extinct for many of the intervening years). The gardens are well worth a visit - parts of them having been laid out by John Tradescant - and even the walled Garden Centre carries some of the grandeur of its situation.

Now, leave The Square to the left of the shady, public garden into Swan Street, past the Old Forge and the gates to the Church of Sts Mary and Bartholomew. The main fabric of the church is of the 13th and 15th Century, with a 15thC tower and pulpit, but the North doorway dates back to the 12thC and there are 14thC wall paintings inside. The church was restored in 1875 when the present chancel was added.

After the Church, carry on to the end of Swan Street where the "Strictly Private" drive leads into the grounds of the Manor House. Veer off right, past a row of cottages, to a Footpath-arrowed stile in the corner and across to an arrowed kissing gate in the wooden fence ahead of you. Through the gate, walk on up to the gravel track and bear left, passing through the avenue of beech trees that leads to the gardens of the Manor House. Now the track has gained a row of fence-protected trees along its left flank and a wire-fenced field on the right. At Manor Farm, zig-zag Lt/Rt after passing through the farm gate across the track which now becomes a tarmac lane. There are brick farm buildings on your right and a tarmac lane goes off over the River Crane on the left. Past the poplars on the LH corner, there is a wire fence and a hedge at the edge of the meadow and, after the cottage on your right, the lane bends slightly. Then a wide entrance to the low field across the river is faced by a "No Right of Way" sign. Keep straight on, past the wide track/Footpath on your right, after which a lay-by and a cattle trough stand opposite a small, derelict barn in a hedged, abandoned orchard. Carry on past two gates into the RH field and through a pair of gates across your path. Now, with Cranborne Dairy Farm house and garden on your left, turn right in the wide area ahead, skirting round the storage tank on the near RH corner. Go across to the small gate signed "Please Shut the Gate" next to two corner field gates. This is where the Route 2 walkers come back to join you on Route 3 - Stage 3.

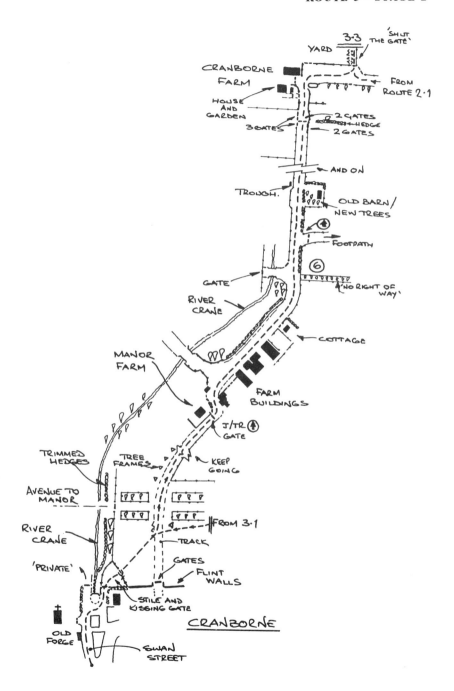

CRANBORNE DAIRY FARM TO SQUIRRELS CORNER

Through the small gate, you will find an excavated farmyard on your left and a wire fence on your right. Follow the path to the iron gate at the other end and turn left through the gate to keep encircling the yard which is now fenced-in as well as banked. Past the LH turn into the yard, signed "No Right of Way", go over the stile next to the gates in the wooden fencing at the bottom of your track. Turn left into the very wide area which is a mass of wooden fencing and farm gates with a wire fence bounding the field on your right. Follow the wire fence round, with barns, silage tanks and outbuildings of Cranborne Dairy Farm on your left, dropping down to ford the River Crane. This is where you need the plastic bags because, due to the clarity of this chalk stream, it's deeper than it looks and the wire fence that crosses it won't support you. Just slip them over your boots and all will be well. A little footbridge would be most appreciated just here.

Now, shake the water of your bags and veer off to the right to find the Bridleway-signed farm gate in the wire fence across your path. The field beyond this gate slopes up to fenced-in trees on your left whilst the River Crane flows along the tree line on your right. Follow the grassy track up to a farm gate and a smaller gate next to it, also Bridleway-arrowed, and the field still slopes down from left to right as you ascend. The uphill track is not so distinct after the gate but it is clear enough to follow as it wends its way up to another small gate to the left of a pair of farm gates in the top LH corner of the field. Through this gate, you emerge onto a wide entrance with a plethora of gates and a stile right next to the busy B3081. Carefully cross the B3081 to the high verge opposite and turn right. I know you're meant to face the oncoming traffic but the verge on that side soon becomes impassable and it's not safe to walk along this road. It's too busy and a soft verge of long grass is safer than the road.

You will have noticed that your map runs out here and joins Route 1 - Stage 6 but, if you turn to it, you'll wonder why you bothered because it's only a few hundred yards from here to the end - along the road verge. So I'll summarize here what it says on Route 1 - Stage 6:

Keep straight on, with a hedged field and views across the valley to where you reached Cursus Gate earlier today over on your right. After a few more yards, the field on your left gives way to mixed pine and deciduous woodland and a wooden barrier into the woods warns "Private. Keep Out". Follow the verge for 200 yards and then turn into the well-used parking area where you started the Day's walk. And don't forget, there are several more walks that you can do from here including Route 4 which takes you in the opposite direction completely.

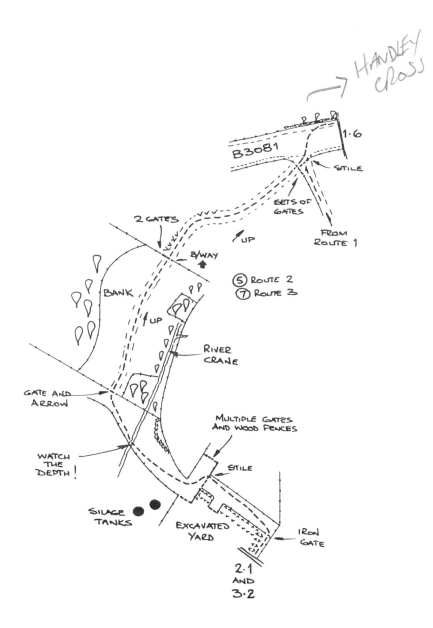

ROUTE 4 - STAGE 1

SQUIRRELS CORNER TO MONKTON UP WIMBORNE

From the parking area, immediately turn down the track into the beech, chestnut and pine woods, away from the B3081. In a few yards, a pair of broken gates face each other across your path, leading onto Private tracks into the woods. You soon arrive in a wide, grassy clearing with a wire-fenced field over on your right with a farm gate at the nearest end and a couple of pine trees where the clearing narrows again into your track. There are no Bridleway signs along here but this farm track is free to use as a Bridleway - fear not.

This hedged, downward slope leads you round a couple of bends, with the bank high on your left and the field dropping away on your right, to an opening into the LH field and a pair of holly bushes in a dip. The grass-centred track rises slightly and, after openings into two RH fields, keeps descending with high fields on the left and a dip down into the fields on the right, past opposite field entrances, a high hedge on the left and more openings before a LH bend.

This particular track should be kept in mind when you start the return trip on the Ackling Dyke in a few minutes time as there couldn't be a greater contrast in route-making than these two diverse ways - one constructed as a military, marching road and the other winding as it will across identical landscape but with no urgency. I know which feels more relaxing, even without the occurrence on the Ackling Dyke. Oh! I haven't told you about that yet, have I?

Anyway, you now have confirmation that this is a true Bridleway - two posts, one either side of the track, carry "Bridleway" arrows on their far side. More openings on your LH side lead into the high fields and a hedged track on your right descends to the barns and farmyard of Manor Farm, Monkton Up Wimborne. As you arrive, between young beeches in the high hedges on both sides of the track, at a T-junction, turn right onto the tarmac road which comes from Wimborne St Giles on your left. The River Allen runs through the meadow field facing you as you turn around the hedged and fenced garden of Manor Farm.

Manor Farm, Monkton Up Wimborne

142

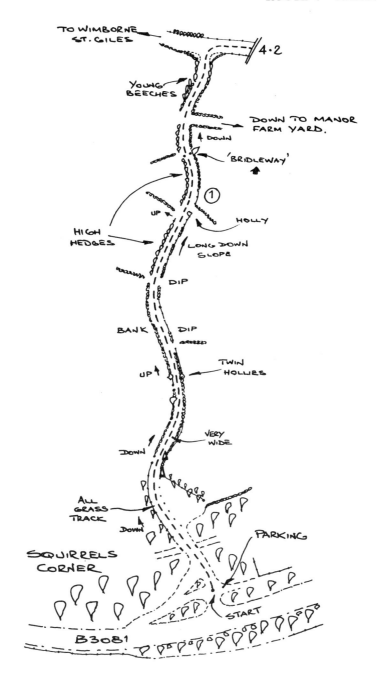

ROUTE 4 - STAGE 2

MONKTON UP WIMBORNE TO HARLEY WOOD

The nice, level tarmac doesn't last long - on your route, anyway. Only as you pass Manor Farm, with its fine stone and flint chequered chimney breast, and the post box on the corner of the wooden fence. As the lane continues between hedges, turn left onto the much-used Bridleway (no signs) and, passing a farm gate into the field on your left, go through the cantilever gate across your path. The young chalk-stream which flows under the bridge is the River Allen, just setting off to flow through some glorious meadowland all the way to Wimborne where it joins the River Stour. The track is now raised on a hedged and fenced causeway to keep it clear of wet-weather flooding and, as a signposted Footpath goes off to your left at an S-bend, the track climbs steeply between banked hedges of beech and hawthorn with loose flints underfoot but with grass up the middle.

At a wide opening on your left, you will see a new plantation in the high field and there is another opening into the field on your right. You still have the young beeches growing in the high hedges as you reach a junction with your main track bearing round to the left. With a vast, wire-fenced field facing you, turn right instead onto a long, pebbly track. There are still no Footpath or Bridleway signs but this is a Bridleway. As you stroll along this track, high up on Harley Down, there are several specimen trees planted in the wide, double hedge on your right and the field on your left slopes away downhill. The fence soon becomes broken and interspersed with sparse hawthorns and, after a while, you will have fine views through the first opening in the RH hedge to Pentridge Hill in the distance. If you intend to extend your walk after Route 4, you will have the conquest and exploration of Pentridge Hill in mind for later today.

Just past this opening, there is (or, at least, there was) a pile of cut logs on the right and it was here that I saw a stoat weaving in and out of the logpile. This isn't as irrelevant a statement as it may appear because stoats are the greatest enemy of rabbits and hares and there presence could greatly affect the prophecy of Armageddon which I mentioned way back in the conclusion of Routes 1 to 3 on Route 1 - Stage 6.

But, before we come to that, just press on, past a couple more openings in the hedge on your right, past a Bridleway arrow (at last) by a track that goes off to your left, into a narrow strip of beech and sycamore woodland known as 'Harley Wood'. In the woods, a track turns off right but ignore it and keep straight on through to a crossing of Bridleways. Turn right here, where there is a memorial stone on the left of the cutting for John Ironmonger 1919-1980 and three Bridleway arrows on the far corner, onto the Bridleway which runs between the LH bank and the RH strip of woodland.

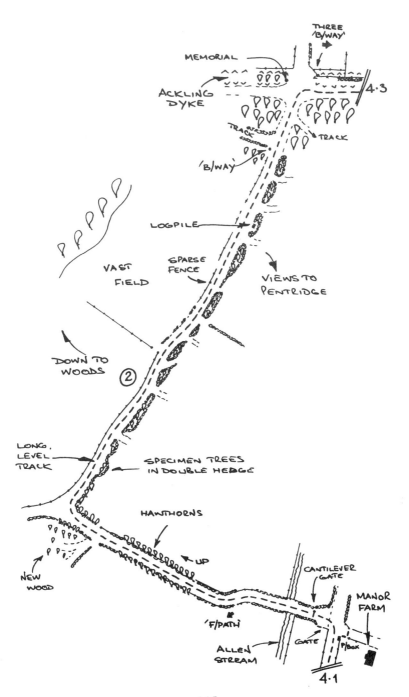

THREE
'B/WAY'

MEMORIAL

ACKLING
DYKE

4.3

TRACK

TRACK

'B/WAY'

LOGPILE

SPARSE
FENCE

VAST
FIELD

VIEWS TO
PENTRIDGE

DOWN TO
WOODS

②

LONG,
LEVEL
TRACK

SPECIMEN TREES
IN DOUBLE HEDGE

HAWTHORNS

UP

NEW
WOOD

CANTILEVER
GATE

MANOR
FARM

'F/PATH'

GATE

P/BOX

ALLEN
STREAM

4.1

145

ROUTE 4 - STAGE 3

HARLEY WOOD TO BOTTLEBUSH DOWN

Just before you turn up onto the top of Ackling Dyke - for this is what the embankment is - let me tell you why the stoat was so significant on Stage 2. An old Dorset rhyme insists that,

"When Cranborne is whoreless, Wimborne is poorless
and Harley Wood is hareless, the world will be at an end"

It would be unethical to comment on the first part and too socially incorrect to comment on the second part, so I'll just worry about the hares.

Actually, there's more to worry about as your path zig-zags left onto the top of the Dyke, with the woods down on your right and a fenced field down on your left. The last time I walked down this part of the Roman Ackling Dyke, a route also used by Saxons and Normans and the scene of many localized disputes during the Bronze and Iron ages, it was a warm, sunny and windless day and I was enjoying the shade from the overhanging trees. Suddenly, I felt a firm slap on my right shoulder but, when I turned round in surprise, there was nobody there. I looked on the ground to see whether some broken branch had dropped onto my shoulder, but there was nothing on the ground. I looked to make sure that I hadn't walked into a low branch - and there wasn't a low branch. I still have no explanation for the slap on the shoulder and I don't like to conjecture too much.

Anyway, continue your gentle, downhill stroll until you reach a clearing and the Dyke becomes flattened on its right flank. Our route passes a Bridleway arrow and then crosses the Monkton Up Wimborne road. Cross over and continue straight on, now with the Dyke submerged in trees on the left of the track and with new trees growing on the right. The path is grassy and long but made difficult for walkers by the deep hoofprints hidden in the long grass.

The Dyke is now above head height as a track crosses your path and cuts straight through the Dyke into an open field beyond its banks. In this field, on Wyke Down, there are some fine Bronze age tumuli which stand proudly above the grass or crops.

Continue along the edge of the Dyke as the track soon widens, with the woods going away slightly to the right and with our path bending towards the Dyke after crossing another track which meets us from the right and goes over the Dyke into the tumuli field. Bending left and right to follow the Dyke's path, the track now runs between the RH wire fence and the Dyke but, after the first few yards, the grass tends to get a bit dense so go up onto the top of the Dyke where you will find a strangely carved stone and a thin path weaving its way between staggered hawthorns. Along the way, there are fine views from the top of the Dyke and, after two cuttings through it, come down again at a clearing with two gates. Carefully cross the B3081 to the surprisingly placed apple tree and join Route 1 - Stage 2 to extend your walk or return along the verge to the parking area at Squirrels Corner where you started, by reversing down the first part of the Route 1 - Stage 2 map.

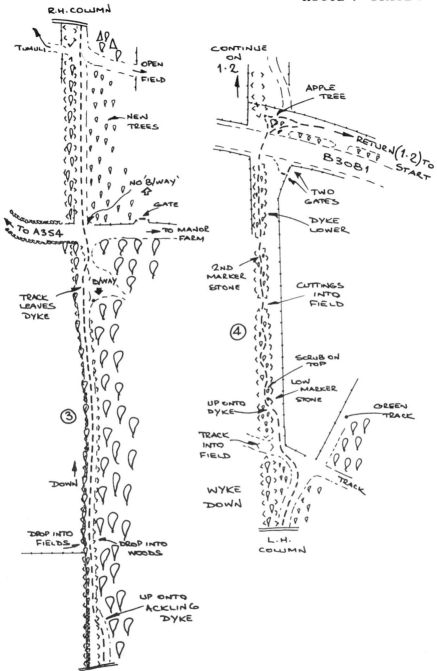

R.H. COLUMN

TUMULI

OPEN FIELD

NEW TREES

NO 'B/WAY'

GATE

TO A354

TO MANOR FARM

TRACK LEAVES DYKE

B/WAY

③

DOWN

DROP INTO FIELDS

DROP INTO WOODS

UP ONTO ACKLING DYKE

4·2

CONTINUE ON 1·2

APPLE TREE

RETURN (1·2) TO START

B3081

TWO GATES

DYKE LOWER

2ND MARKER STONE

CUTTINGS INTO FIELD

④

SCRUB ON TOP

LOW MARKER STONE

UP ONTO DYKE

GREEN TRACK

TRACK INTO FIELD

TRACK

WYKE DOWN

L.H. COLUMN

IN CONCLUSION

After such a breathtaking exploration of this beautiful county, where can I start with an appreciation of the splendours we have seen - or will see, if you're reading this before you even set foot outside? I didn't undertake these walks in the order in which they appear in the book and I don't expect that you will either. After each one, I thought that I must have seen the best that Dorset has to offer. Then I did another one and had the same thoughts all over again.

I have to confess that I got lost, or at least had a little difficulty in finding the right way, on several occasions but the detailed Stage maps show the right ways and the additional advice should have made certain that you found your way alright. I think the least helpful area where Footpath arrows are concerned has to be the Ilchester estate and farms but, now that all of the defects have been reported to Dorset County Council Rights of Way Section, these have been or, hopefully, will be corrected very soon. However, as I found all of the right ways through, the book should have saved you having any similar problems.

I have tried to evaluate which were the best parts of all of these walks but, on reflection, it is impossible to say categorically, "This ridge walk with its superb views of the sea or vast, lonely downland was definitely the best" or "That tiny church nestling in a sunny, bird song-filled valley was the most beautiful" or "This or that fine country house in its magnificent park was the high spot of the walk". However, if pressed, I would probably choose the view from Swyre Head on the Encombe walk as embodying most of what Dorset is all about. From the ridge, the view encompasses fine, expansive coastal and cliff scenery, a pattern of farmland and a fine stone country house in the valley (with another one in the valley behind). There is a little, thatched village and church in the distance and a folly on the cliff top. On top of all that, rooks are arguing in the woods, hordes of sheep are quietly devouring the rough grass and skylarks are chattering above. It's a bit of heaven.

However, Bottlebush Down and Pentridge Hill take some beating and I'm delighted to have found Melbury Sampford park and Chantmarle - and the lovely little churches of Melbury Bubb and Frome St Quintin. The trio of pretty villages on the Stour Valley excursion provided three enchanting corners to a wonderful meadow and farmland exploration along my favourite river whilst the villages of Ashmore and Compton Abbas were perfect foils to an intriguing ramble through ancient woods and over high downs with magnificent views (Spreadeagle Hill and the Melbury and Fontmell Downs were brilliant, weren't they?) rivalling my original choice of Swyre Head.

And what can I say about Abbotsbury and the Gorwell Farm excursion? The ridge walk was wonderful and the dairy farm valley by The Grey Mare and Her Colts was so far removed from the well-visited village of Abbotsbury and St Catherine's Chapel as to feel strangely remote and peaceful whilst the ancient woods were, again, filled with bird song. The high ridge views of Chesil Beach and Portland were well worth the climb whilst the stroll near the sea, on the way to the Chapel, was very pleasant indeed. The walk from Wimborne to Badbury Rings and around Kingston Lacy park was fascinating and quite an easy introduction to these guided walks. For all that, my enduring memory is that this was the greenest walk with leafy trees, fine views from Badbury Rings and the lovely village green at Pamphill on the way back.

I'll have to leave you to make up your own minds, but don't do it until you've been on all of the walks.

BIBLIOGRAPHY

History and Antiquities of the County of Dorset: Rev John Hutchins 1861 - 64

Inventory of Historical Monuments in the County of Dorset: H.M.S.O. 1970

Dorset Churches: Sir Owen Morshead: Dorset Historic Churches Trust 1976

The Place Names of Dorset - Parts 2 and 3: A D Mills of the English Place Names
    Society - Edited by K Cameron.

Dorset Barrows: Leslie Grinsell F S A

Portrait of Dorset: Ralph Wightman: Robert Hale

The Old Roads of Dorset: Ronald Good

Inside Dorset: Monica Hutchings 1964

Unknown Dorset: D Maxwell 1927

Geology Explained in Dorset: John W Perkins: David and Charles

Geology and Scenery in England and Wales: A E Truman: Pelican Books

Gardeners' Encyclopedia of Plants and Flowers: Christopher Brickell: R H S

Ashmore - A History of the Parish with Index Registers 1651-1820: E W Watson
    M.A. of the Society of St Andrew, Salisbury 1890

Cranborne Chase: Desmond Hawkins: Victor Gollancz 1980

A Chronicle of Cranborne and Cranborne Chase: T W Wake Smart 1841

Purbeck Shop: Eric Benfield: Ensign Publications

Dorset Upalong and Downalong: W.I. Members 1935 - Ed by Marianne Dacombe

ACKNOWLEDGMENTS

Thanks again to my wife Janet for listening to my theories about landscape formation
and then putting me straight on the geology. Thanks for providing me with some
wonderful picnics for my diurnal meanderings and for being a guinea-pig on some of
my new walks. Thanks to my son Harvey for the tale of the Chantmarle poacher.
There were more stories of this area but space was a bit short - *this time.*

Thanks to all the staff at Lansdowne Reference Library, Bournemouth who frequently
delved into the Dorset archives to retrieve some dusty tome or other. Thanks to the
Local Studies Librarian at Dorchester County Library for finding the more ancient and
remote items and finally, thanks to Barry Thomas and Phil Drake of the Dorset Rights
of Way Section for sorting out problems at Compton Abbas and the Evershot area.

A37.   104,106,108
A350. 36
A354. 121,136
Abbot Street, Pamphill. 26
Abbotsbury. 56,64,70,72,80,100
      Castle. 56,66
      Castle, 2nd. 70
      Sub-Tropical Gardens. 70
Ackling Dyke. 20,124,126,142,146
Alcester Abbey. 16
Aldhelm's Head, St. 96
Alfred the Great. 8
Alley Moor, Gorwell. 62
All Fools Lane, Cowgrove. 26
Armada, Spanish. 66
Arundell, Roger. 100
Ashmore. 30,40,42

B3081. 120,123,128,132,138,142,146
B3082. 18,20,22,24,30
B3157. 66
Back Lane, Abbotsbury. 58
Back Lane, Evershot. 110
Badbury Rings. 14,18,20,22,24
Bankes, Arabella. 12
      , John. 12,26
      , Lady F I. 78
      , Ralph. 12,26,28
      , William. 26
Bankes' Estate. 24
Barry, Charles. 26
Barnsley. 14
Bathan. 20
Beethall, Matthew. 28
Belt, The, Encombe. 80
Berwick St John. 52
Bexington, East, Dairy House.68
      , West. 60,66,68
Bindon Abbey, Wareham. 112
Bishop Close, Abbotsbury. 58
Blackbush Down. 130
Blackmore Vale. 30
Blandford Forum. 36,44
Blind Lane, Abbotsbury. 57,64
Bottlebush Down. 124,126,146
Bow Coppice, Gorwell. 62
Bowldish Pond. 130,132
Bramble Coppice, Gorwell. 62
Bravel. Rector St Mary's. 46

Brickyard Copse, Evershot. 104
Bridport. 64
Broad Coppice, Gorwell. 62
Bubb Down. 106
      Plantation. 106,108
Burton Street, Marnhull. 48,49,50

Cambridge. Kings College. 54
Catley Copse. 10
Cecil, Robert. 138
Cerne, Abbot William. 72
Chantmarle. 112,114,116
      , John. 112
      , Robert. 112
Chapel Lane, Wimborne. 8
Chapmans Pool. 90,94
Charles I. 26
Chesil Beach. 56,58,64,68,70
Chilbridge Farm. 16,18
Christchurch. 24
Church Hill, Marnhull. 49
Churches:
      Steeple. 84
      St Catherine, Abbotsbury. 56,70,72
      St Cuthburga, Wimborne. 8
      St Edwold. 104
      St Gregory, Marnhull. 49
      St James, Kingston. 78
      St Mary, Compton Abbas. 32
      St Mary, Frome St Quintin. 114
      St Mary Magdalene, Fifehead. 50,52
      St Mary the Virgin. 106
      St Michael, Stour Provost. 52
      St Nicholas, Abbotsbury. 52
      St Nicholas, Ashmore. 40
      St Nicholas, Kimmeridge. 84,86
      St Osmund, Melbury Osmond. 102
      St Stephen, Pamphill. 28
Christchurch Harbour. 132
Civil War. 46
Clavell, John (Richards). 90
      , Sir William. 75,88,92
Clavell's Hard. 90,92
      Tower. 90
Clubmen, Dorset. 46
Common, The, Evershot. 118
Compton Abbas. 32,36,38,46
      Airfield. 32,38,40
      , East. 32,34,36

Compton Down. 32
Cooks Row, Wimborne. 30
Corfe Castle. 24,26,78
Cornmarket, Wimborne. 30
Cowgrove. 26,28
Cranborne. 132,134,136,138
    Abbey. 138
    Chase. 32,40,120
Creech Arch. 84
Cromwell. 26,46
Crown and Anchor, Wimborne. 8
Cursus Gate. 126,128,138

Deans Court, Wimborne. 8
Dorchester. 20,22
Dorset Cursus. 124,126
Drive End, Melbury Sampford. 104
Drove Road, Cranborne. 130,134,136
Druid Oaks. 20
Dunford's, Marnhull. 49
Durnovaria (Dorchester). 20
Durotriges. 22

East Borough, Wimborne. 8
East Compton. 32,34,36
Elizabeth I. 138
Elizabeth II. 36
Eldon, Earls of. 78,80,94
Eldon's Seat. 94
Encombe Estate. 75,78,94,96
    House. 76,78,80,94
English Channel. 132
Ethelred. 8
Evershot. 98,100,108,110,116,118
Exeter. 22

Farms:
    Barn Dairy, Smedmore. 88
    Bexington, East. 56,68
    Bridge, Melbury Osmond. 102
    Burl, Evershot. 116,118
    Chilbridge, Wimborne. 16,18
    Church, Melbury Bubb. 104,106
    Cranborne Dairy. 134,136,138,140
    Fortuneswood, Evershot. 110,112
    Gorwell, at Gorwell. 56,57,60,62
    Hazel, Melbury Sampford. 108
    Lodge, Melbury Sampford. 100
    Kimmeridge. 86
    Manor, Ashmore. 40
    Manor, Cranborne. 138
    Manor, Monkton Up Wimb'ne. 142,144
    Manor, Pamphill. 26

Nash Court, Marnhull. 54
Old Dairy, Compton Abbas. 36
Swalland, Smedmore. 76,82
West Wood, Evershot. 110,116
Fifehead Magdalen. 48,50,52
Fillymead, Marnhull. 49
Fitch, John. 12
    , William. 12
Fleet Nature Reserve. 70
Fleetwood, Colonel. 46
Folly Hanging Gate, Ashmore. 44
Fontmell Down. 32,36,38,44,46
Fontmell Magna. 46
Fontmell Wood. 32
Fore Street, Evershot. 110
Fore Top. 38,46
Fox-Strangways. 56
Frome St Quintin. 114,116
Fudge, Mrs. Marnhull. 49

Gad Cliff. 84
Gappergennies. 44
Gibson, John. Stour Provost. 48,52
Gillingham, Roger. 28
Gilly, Samuel. 12
Giraldus, Abbot. 138
Glastonbury. 128
Gore Clump. 38
Great Morris Close, Ashmore. 42
Grey Mare and Her Colts. 56,60
Grove Field, Marnhull. 49
Gussage Hill. 124

Haims Lane, Marnhull. 50,54
Halfpenny Lane, Ashmore. 42
Hambledon Hill. 34,46
Hamworthy, Poole. 30
Hanham Road, Wimborne. 8
Hardy Monument. 58,66
Hardy, Thomas. 114
Hardy, Thomas Masterman. 58
Harley Wood. 144,146
Hazel Wood, Melbury Sampford. 108
Henry VIII. 100
High Hall. 12,14
Highways Act. 2
Holywell, Evershot. 116
Houns Tout. 75,76,94,96
Hugh, Earl. 52

Ilchester Arms, Abbotsbury. 56,58,72
Ilchester, Earls of. 56,98
Ina, King of West Saxons. 8

Ironmonger, John. 144

James I. 138
John, King. 112,138

Kimmeridge. 75,76,84,86,88
    Bay. 90
King Down Wood. 14,18,20
Kings College, Cambridge. 54
Kingston. 75,76,78,96
Kingston Lacy. 12,16,18,24
Kingston Russell Stone Circle. 60
Knobcrook Lane, Wimborne. 8

Leland. 20
Llewelyn, Derek. Stour Provost. 52
Lodge Farm Kingston Lacy. 16,18,24
London. 22
    , Great Fire of. 12
Longcombe Bottom. 46
Love Lane, Marnhull. 50,54

Maber, Sara. 114
Maiden Castle, Dorchester. 20
Manswood. 16
Market Street, Abbotsbury. 56
Marnhull. 48,49,50,54
Martin. 136
    Down. 124
Mansel of Smedmore. 86
Martin. 8
Maximinus, Emperor. 72
Melbury Beacon. 34,46
    Down. 34
    Hill. 34
Melbury Bubb. 102,106
Melbury Osmond. 102,104
Melbury Park, Evershot. 100,102,104,
    110
Melbury Sampford. 100,102
Monk, William. 52
Monkton Up Wimborne. 142,144,146
Moriconium, Poole. 30

Nash Court, Marnhull. 49,54
    Villa. 54
Nelson, Lord. 58
Newman, Sir Richard. 52
    , Thomas. 52
Nine Barrow Down. 78

Oakley Down, Wimborne St Giles. 126
Okeford Hill. 66

Old Road, Wimborne. 30

Pamphill. 26,28
    Dairy Farm Shop. 6,28
Park Coppice, Gorwell. 60,62
Penbury Knoll. 128
Pentridge. 121,128,130,132,144
Pitt, George. 80
    , John. 80
    , William Moreton. 80
Plantation, The, Kingston. 75,78,96
Polar Wood, Encombe. 80
Poole. 30,138
Ponting, C E. 28
Portesham. 58
Portland. 58,64
Pratt, Sir Roger. 26
Priaulx, Monastery. 54
Priors Walk, Wimborne. 8
Pudding and Pye, Wimborne. 30
Purbeck, Isle of. 75

Repton, Lady E. 94
Richards, Rev John. 90
Rights of Way Act. 2
Rivers:
    Allen. 12,16,140,144
    Crane. 128,132,138
    Frome. 110,112,114
    Stour. 8,24,28,30,34,48,49,50,52,
        132,144
    Wim (Wym). 8
Rope Head Lake. 82,92,94

Sackmore Lane, Marnhull. 48,49,50
Saints:
    St Aldhelm's Head. 96
    St Catherine (Chapel). 56,72
    St Cuthburga, Wimborne. 8
    St Edwold, Melbury Bubb. 104
    St Gregory, Marnhull. 49
    St James, Kingston. 78
    St John (Spring), Evershot. 110
    St Mary, Compton Abbas. 32
    St Mary, Frome St Quintin. 114
    St Mary Magdalen, Fifehead. 50,52
    St Mary the Virgin, Melbury Bubb. 106
    St Michael, Stour Provost. 52
    St Nicholas, Ashmore. 4
    St Nicholas, Abbotsbury. 56
    St Nicholas, Kimmeridge. 84,86
    St Osmund, Melbury Osmond. 102
    St Stephen, Pamphill. 28

Salisbury. 16,22,138
, Earl of. 138
Salisbury Plantation. 126
Salisbury Street, Cranborne. 136
School Corner, Evershot. 110
School Lane, Wimborne. 8
Scott Arms, Kingston. 75,78,96
Scott, John. 78,80
, Sir William. 78
Seven Taps, Kimmeridge. 86,88
Shaftesbury. 36,44,46,78
Shakespeare Road, Wimborne. 10
Shapwick. 24
Shepherds Bottom, Ashmore. 32,40,44
Sherborne. 34
Short family, Lodge Farm. 18
Smedmore Hill. 75,76,80,82
House. 82,86,88
South Street, Kingston. 78
Spanish Armada. 66
Spinneys Pond, Ashmore. 44
Spreadeagle Hill. 32,34,38,44
Square, The, Cranborne. 138
Squirrels Corner, Cranborne. 121,123,
124,130,132,134,136,140,146
Stock Wood, Melbury Bubb. 106
Stockwood Common. 104
Stone Lane, Wimborne. 8
Stour Provost. 48,52,54
Mill. 52
Stourhead. 24,49
Stourton. 49
Stowell, Baron. 78
Strangways. 56,80
, Dorothy. 102
, Eleanor. 100
, Giles. 100
, Henry. 100
, Thomas. 100
Strangways-Horner, Susanna. 102
Stratfieldsaye. 80
Street, G E, Arch. 78
Strode, John. 112
Stubhampton Bottom. 42
Sturminster Marshall. 22
Sturminster Newton. 34
Summer Lane, Evershot. 110
Swalland Field. 82,92

Swan, The., Abbotsbury. 56
Swan Street, Cranborne. 138
Sweetbriar Drove, Shapwick. 18,24
Swyre Head. 75,76,80,82,92
Wood. 80

Tewkesbury, Abbey. 138
Thorpe, Abbot Henry de. 72
Toby's Bottom. 130,134,136
Todber. 49
Tourist Information, Wimborne. 6
Toyd Down. 136
Tradescant, John. 138
Trafalgar, Battle of. 58
Trill Bridge, Stour Provost. 54
Turks Hill. 66,68
Turnpike, Great Western. 120,124,136,
138
Tyneham. 84

Vagg, John. 114
Vespasian. 22
Vectis - Isle of Wight. 22
Victoria Road, Wimborne. 30
Vine Hill, Pamphill. 28

Walford Bridge, Wimborne. 8
Walford Mill. 8
Washers Pit. 32,40,42,44
Wear Hill, Abbotsbury. 57,62,64,66
Welcome Inn, The. Evershot. 104
Wellington, Duke of. 80
West Bay. 64
West Bexington. 60,66,68
West Hill, Evershot. 100
West Stour. 52
West Street, Abbotsbury. 72
, Kingston. 78
, Wimborne. 30
West Wood, Ashmore. 32,34,40,46
White Hart, Wimborne. 30
White Hill, Abbotsbury. 58,60
Wight, Isle of (Vectis). 22
William the Conqueror. 78
Wilksworth Caravan Park. 10
Wimborne Minster. 6,12,30,144
Wimborne St Giles. 126,142
Witchampton. 16

13/9/02 FRIDAY

WALKED BOTTLEBRUSH ROUND SECT. 1/2/3
WEATHER BEAUTIFUL 22/23 DEGS. ON FINISHING SECT 3
I TURNED LEFT INSTEAD OF RIGHT THEREFORE MISSING BUS To
SALISBURY AT HANDLEY CROSS ROUNDABOUT.
